D0368709

LANDMARK SUPREME COURT
DECISIONS
ON
PUBLIC SCHOOL ISSUES

by

Edward C. Bolmeier

Emeritus Professor of Education
Duke University

THE MICHIE COMPANY
Law Publishers
CHARLOTTESVILLE, VIRGINIA

PREFACE

The American citizenry should be thoroughly enlightened as to the judicial system of our Federal Government. This is especially true with respect to the purposes and functioning of the United States Supreme Court on school matters.

Many persons are inclined to launch criticism and condemnations against the Court because of its decisions on school issues which are in conflict with their subjective opinions. It is doubtful though that, in so doing, they first consult the actual official opinions of the Court. Too often the critics rely upon comments of news media and others for sources of information—much of which may be made for influential purposes. This is most manifest on the very controversial issues concerning religious influences and racial desegregation in the public schools—and particularly during a campaign period when political holders and aspirants are seeking the support of voters by making critical references to the High Court and its decisions in order to solicit such support.

Of course the great majority of students, teachers, and other citizens are interested in obtaining *objective information* concerning the *landmark decisions* rendered by the United States Supreme Court. Unfortunately not all have ready access to the law reporters in which the complete and official opinions of the Court are reported.

Therefore it is the purpose of this publication to

present, in concise form, the most significant information concerning the landmark decisions for the entire period (1923-1972) in which the Supreme Court has rendered decisions on school issues.

Not every Supreme Court decision on school issues has been included in this report. The selection includes only those which have caused the greatest public concern and controversy. Many of them have established legal principles which may serve as guidelines for other potential litigation on forthcoming questions in which constitutionality is involved.

E.C.B.

Durham, North Carolina
April 1973

CONTENTS

CONTENTS

Chapter 1

INTRODUCTION

The Constitution of the United States provides for the establishment and functioning of three branches of the federal government. Article I provides for the *legislative* branch (Congress); Article II refers to the *executive* branch; and Article III deals with the *judicial* branch.

Each of these three branches of government assumes authority and performs functions which have significant bearings on the school. However, in recent years, much more public attention has been focused on the judicial branch of the federal government than on either of the other two branches in matters concerning the schools. Also more criticism has been launched against this branch of government because of the manner and degree in which it has assumed its constitutional obligations for the protection of rights and liberties in school situations. Before carrying the criticism of the federal judiciary to extremes it is well to scrutinize (1) the system of federal courts as provided for in the Constitution, (2) the processes by which the courts carry out their constitutional mandate, and (3) the reported reasoning of the courts for the decisions rendered in disputed school cases.

System of Federal Courts

Article III, Section I of the Constitution of the

United States provides that the "judicial Power of the United States, shall be vested in one supreme Court, and in such inferior Courts as the Congress may from time to time ordain and establish."

This constitutional provision places the Supreme Court at the pinnacle in the judicial hierarchy as the ultimate repository of judicial power. As its title implies it is "supreme" as the judicial authority.

Immediately below the Supreme Court in authority are the courts of appeals (circuit courts). The United States is divided into ten judicial circuits, plus the District of Columbia as an additional circuit. In each of these circuits is a United States court of appeals. Each of the states is assigned to one of the circuits.

The purpose of the circuit courts is to relieve the Supreme Court of considering all appeals in cases originally decided by the federal trial courts. They are empowered to review all final decisions of district courts, except in very rare instances in which the law provides for the direct review by the Supreme Court.

Next in line of authority immediately below the appellate courts are the United States district courts. These courts are the trial courts with general federal jurisdiction. Each state has at least one district court, while some of the more populous states have as many as four. Altogether there are 88 district courts serving the 50 states and the District of Columbia.

"Cases from the district courts are reviewed by the United States courts of appeals except that injunction orders of 3-judge district courts, certain decisions holding acts of Congress unconstitutional, and certain criminal decisions may be appealed directly to the Supreme Court." (United States Government Organization Manual—1970-71, p. 46)

Jurisdiction of the Supreme Court

Since 1789, when the Constitution was ratified, Congress has made a variety of "exceptions" and "regulations" governing the appellate jurisdiction of the Supreme Court. This is an important congressional power for the reason that, while Congress cannot expand or extend the jurisdiction of the Supreme Court beyond the limits set by the Constitution, it can impose restrictions and requirements within the limits set by the Constitution.

In broad terms, the Supreme Court is given jurisdiction by Congress to review: (1) all cases in lower federal courts, and (2) all cases in state courts in which there is involved a question of the meaning or effect of a federal statute or a constitutional provision.

Before reviewing school cases which have been decided by the Supreme Court, consideration should be given to the procedural methods by which the vast number of federal and state cases which are potentially appealable are sifted by the Supreme Court in order to reduce the number of cases actually brought before the Court. There are two methods: (1) the *writ of certiorari*, and (2) *appeal*.

The *writ of certiorari* is an order issued by a higher tribunal to an inferior body ordering it to certify up to it the record of a case before the inferior court. Certiorari is obtained in the case of the United States Supreme Court upon petition to the Court by the parties.

Appeal is the second method of obtaining review by the Supreme Court of a lower court case. This is handled by a party filing a jurisdictional statement which sets forth the reasons why the case qualifies for Supreme Court review and why it has sufficient merit to warrant further hearings by the Supreme Court.

By these procedural techniques the Supreme Court gives preliminary scrutiny to every case coming to it to determine whether further action by the Court is warranted. The effectiveness of this system is attested by the fact that nearly 90 per cent of all cases submitted to the Supreme Court are disposed of without argument.

Despite the procedural techniques of minimizing the number of cases to be decided by the Court, the demands made upon the high tribunal are still excessive. With the growing controversy over human rights, and especially since the enactment of the Civil Rights Act in 1964, the burden imposed upon the United States Supreme Court has grown to the point where more measures need to be taken for relief.

Since much of the responsibility of the Supreme

Court has to do with the *judicial review of legislation*, attempts were made a quarter of a century ago to limit entertaining cases in that area. In a concurring opinion Justice Brandeis enumerated certain rules of the Court governing judicial review of legislation as follows:

1. The Court will not pass upon the constitutionality of legislation in a friendly, non-adversary, proceeding, declining because to decide such questions is legitimate only in the last resort, and as a necessity in the determination of real, earnest and vital controversy between individuals.

2. The Court will not anticipate a question of constitutional law in advance of the necessity of deciding it. . . . It is not the habit of the Court to decide questions of a constitutional nature unless absolutely necessary to a decision of the case.

3. The Court will not formulate a rule of constitutional law broader than is required by the precise facts to which it is to be applied.

4. The Court will not pass upon a constitutional question although properly presented by the record, if there is also present some other ground upon which the case may be disposed of.

5. The Court will not pass upon the validity of a statute upon complaint of one who fails to show that he is injured by its operation.

6. The Court will not pass upon the constitutionality of a statute at the instance of one who has availed himself of its benefits. (*Ashwander* v. *Tennessee Valley Authority*, 297 U.S. 288, at 346-48, 1936)

Constitutional Provisions Pertaining to Education

The great majority of school cases reaching the United States Supreme Court are related to the "human rights" provisions of the Constitution, spelled out most specifically in the amendments. The First Amendment and the Fourteenth Amendment have especially been involved in cases dealing with racial discrimination and religion in the schools. Less frequently the Fifth Amendment, dealing with self-incrimination, has been referred to in cases involving alleged subversive affiliations.

Significantly, the First Amendment restrained only the federal government in dealing with human rights. This left the states almost completely free to infringe the most basic human rights in any way their governments might wish. Not until the Fourteenth Amendment was adopted in 1868 did it become possible for the federal courts and Congress to restrict state action governing human life.

Court cases concerning religious instruction in the public schools aptly illustrate the necessary concomitance of the Fourteenth Amendment to restrain the states in matters of human rights.

The First Amendment (1791) stipulates that "Congress shall make no law respecting an establishment of religion, or prohibiting the free exercise thereof. . . ." Conspicuously, the First Amendment applied only to Congress and did not prohibit state legislatures from enacting laws "respecting an establishment of religion or prohibiting the free exercise thereof."

Application of the First Amendment to the states is depicted in the Fourteenth Amendment (1868) as follows:

> All persons born or naturalized in the United States, and subject to the jurisdiction thereof, are citizens of the United States and of the State wherein they reside. No State shall make or enforce any law which shall abridge the privileges or immunities of citizens of the United States; nor shall any State deprive any person of life, liberty or property, without due process of law; nor deny to any person within its jurisdiction the equal protection of the laws.

It follows from this section of the Fourteenth Amendment that it makes national citizenship primary and state citizenship derivative therefrom. "The fundamental concept of liberty embodied in the Fourteenth Amendment embraces the liberties guaranteed by the First Amendment."

Selection of Landmark Decisions

To analyze every United States Supreme Court decision affecting the public schools is beyond the scope of the writer's undertaking. Although only three such decisions were rendered by the High Court during the century, 1789-1888, and 22 more during the period 1889-1948, there has been an accelerated increase during the past several decades.

At the rate the Court has been rendering decisions on school cases recently, and the growing controversy over human rights, it is quite likely that there will be more school decisions rendered during the current 20-year span (1954-1973), than for the entire period preceding.

The scope of this investigation is therefore limited to a selection and treatment of the *most significant* school cases decided by the Supreme Court. The decisions of the cases so selected may be regarded as *landmark decisions.* Admittedly, the selection of "landmark decisions" is rather arbitrary. The very fact that a case has been ruled upon by the highest court in the land makes the decision a "landmark decision."

However, the selection of a limited number of the court decisions—arbitrary though it may be—is based upon several criteria: (1) the extent to which the decision has shaped educational policy; (2) the extent to which the decision has aroused public concern; and (3) the reaction of the other two branches of the federal government on the action taken by the judicial branch.

The selected cases—each one constituting a separate chapter of the book—are presented in chronological order. A determinant in arranging the court decisions chronologically, rather than categorically, is to facilitate periodic supplementation to their publication with forthcoming decisions on school issues as they are rendered by the High Court.

The first case so presented is *Meyer v. Nebraska*

(1923) in which the Supreme Court ruled upon the validity of a statute prohibiting the teaching of German in the public elementary schools. One of the last cases, reported at the time of this writing, is *Wisconsin* v. *Yoder* (1972) which concerns compulsory school attendance laws as applied to Amish people.

Intervening cases, between 1923 and 1972, to be treated, deal with such issues as: free textbooks and transportation for parochial pupils, flag salute requirements, teaching evolution, released time for religious instruction, recitation of prayers, Bible reading, segregation of races in the public schools, academic freedom of teachers, student display of protest insignia, busing of pupils, and parochiaid.

In order to produce the most relevant case information in a simple and uniform fashion, the procedure for the presentation of each case is to indicate: (1) the issue involved, (2) background of the case—including lower court rulings, (3) the United States Supreme Court decision—with selected excerpts from the case reports, and (4) significance and consequences of the decision—as viewed by the writer.

Chapter 2

STATUTORY PROHIBITION TO TEACH GERMAN

(held unconstitutional)

Meyer v. *Nebraska,* 262 U.S. 390,
43 S. Ct. 625 (1923)

The Issue. The question in this case concerned the validity of a state statute forbidding the teaching of modern languages in any school, public, private or parochial, to any child who had not completed the eighth grade.

Background. The law in question was known as the "Siman language law." It was enacted in 1919, following World War I, at a time when the teaching of German was in ill repute. Two other states (Iowa and Ohio) had similar laws. The Nebraska act reads as follows:

> Section 1. No person, individually or as a teacher, shall, in any private, denominational, parochial or public school, teach any subject to any person in any language other than the English language.
>
> Sec. 2. Languages, other than the English language, may be taught as languages only after a pupil shall have attained and successfully passed the eighth grade as evidenced by a certificate of graduation issued by the county superintendent of the county in which the child resides.

Sec. 3. Any person who violates any of the provisions of this act shall be deemed guilty of a misdemeanor and upon conviction, shall be subject to a fine of not less than twenty-five dollars ($25), nor more than one hundred dollars ($100) or be confined in the county jail for any period not exceeding thirty days for each offense.

Sec. 4. Whereas, an emergency exists, this act shall be in force from and after its passage and approval. (262 U.S. at 397)

In violation of the statute, Robert T. Meyer was convicted and fined $25 in a district court for teaching the subject of reading in German language to a child of 10 years, who had not attained and successfully passed the eighth grade. After his conviction, Meyer appealed to the Supreme Court of Nebraska which affirmed the decision of the lower court.

State Supreme Court Decision. In defending its approval of the Nebraska law, and the conviction of the teacher who violated it, the State Supreme Court reasoned that:

The salutary purpose of the statute is clear. The Legislature has seen the baneful effects of permitting foreigners, who had taken residence in this country, to rear and educate their children in the language of their native land. The result of that condition was found to be inimical to our own safety. To allow the children of foreigners, who had emigrated here, to be taught from early childhood the language of the country of their parents was to rear them with that language of their mother tongue. It was to educate them so that they must always think in that language, and, as a consequence, naturally inculcate in them the ideas and sentiments foreign to the best interests of this country. The statute, therefore, was intended not only to require that the education of all children be conducted in the English language, but that, until they had grown into that language and until it had become a part of them, they should not in the schools be taught any other language. The obvious purpose of this statute was that the English language should be and become the mother tongue of all children reared in this state. The enactment of such a statute comes reasonably within the police power of the state.

. . . The Legislature no doubt has in mind the practical operation of the law. The law affects few citizens, except those of foreign lineage. Other citizens, in their selection of studies, except perhaps in rare instances, have never deemed it of importance to teach their children foreign languages before such children have reached the eighth grade. In the legislative mind, the salutary effects of the statute no doubt outweighed the restriction upon the citizens generally, which, it appears, was a restriction of no real consequence. (187 N.W. at 102)

In a dissenting opinion, however, Judge Letton expressed a view which apparently was a factor in appealing the case to the United States Supreme Court. The dissenting judge said, in part:

> ... I am unable to agree with the doctrine that the Legislature may arbitrarily, through the exercise of the police power, interfere with the fundamental right of every American parent to control, in a degree not harmful to the state, the education of his child, and to teach it, in association with other children, any science or art, or any language which contributes to a larger life, or to a higher and broader culture.
>
> Educators agree that the period of early childhood is the time that the ability to speak or understand a foreign, or a classic, language is the most easily acquired. Every parent has the fundamental right, after he has complied with all proper requirements by the state as to education, to give his child such further education in proper subjects as he desires and can afford. (*Id.* at 104)

U. S. Supreme Court Decision. The United States Supreme Court, by a 7 to 2 decision, *reversed the opinion of the Nebraska Supreme Court.* In essence, the decision of the United States Supreme Court was that a statute proscribing the teaching of a modern language below the ninth grade in private or public schools was in violation of the Due Process Clause of the Fourteenth Amendment. The argument that such a regulation fell within the proper police powers of the state was rejected by the High Court.

The majority opinion was delivered by Justice

McReynolds and concurred in by Chief Justice Taft, and Justices McKenna, Van Devanter, Brandeis, Butler and Sanford. Justices Holmes and Sutherland dissented.

Excerpts from the *majority opinion* indicate the Court's reasoning in declaring the Nebraska law unconstitutional:

> Practically, education of the young is only possible in schools conducted by especially qualified persons who devote themselves thereto. The calling always has been regarded as useful and honorable, essential, indeed, to the public welfare. Mere knowledge of the German language cannot reasonably be regarded as harmful. Heretofore it has been commonly looked upon as helpful and desirable. Plaintiff in error taught this language in school as part of his occupation. His right thus to teach and the right of parents to engage him so to instruct their children, we think, are within the liberty of the Amendment. (262 U.S. at 400)
>
> It is said the purpose of the legislation was to promote civic development by inhibiting training and education of the immature in foreign tongues and ideals before they could learn English and acquire American ideals; and that the English language should be and become the mother tongue of all children reared in this State. It is also affirmed that the foreign born population is very large, that certain communities commonly use foreign words, follow foreign leaders, move in a foreign

atmosphere, and that children are thereby hindered from becoming citizens of the most useful type and the public safety is imperiled.

That the State may do much, go very far, indeed, in order to improve the quality of its citizens, physically, mentally and morally, is clear; but the individual has certain fundamental rights which must be respected. The protection of the Constitution extends to all, to those who speak other languages as well as those born with English on the tongue. Perhaps it would be highly advantageous if all had ready understanding of our ordinary speech, but this cannot be coerced by methods which conflict with the Constitution— a desirable end cannot be promoted by prohibited means. (*Id.* at 401)

The desire of the legislature to foster a homogeneous people with American ideals prepared readily to understand current discussions of civic matters is easy to appreciate. Unfortunate experiences during the late war and aversion toward every characteristic of truculent adversaries were certainly enough to quicken that aspiration. But the means adopted, we think, exceed the limitations upon the power of the State and conflict with rights assured to plaintiff in error. The interference is plain enough and no adequate reason therefore in time of peace and domestic tranquility has been shown. (*Id.* at 402)

Significance of the Decision. This was the first and only case concerning the school curriculum to be ruled upon by the United States Supreme Court, other than those in which religion was a factor. (As subsequent cases to be reported in this publication will indicate, the Supreme Court has ruled upon such issues as recitation of prayers and Bible reading because of their relation to the "establishment of religion" clause of the First Amendment. Less directly, other cases with religious overtones, such as those pertaining to the flag salute requirement and the prohibition of teaching the theory of evolution, have been decided by the Supreme Court.)

This case, however, was not considered because of the religious restrictions embodied in the First Amendment, but, rather upon the "due process of law" clause of the Fourteenth Amendment.

In essence the Court made it clear that the Nebraska law interfered with (1) the professional calling of modern-language teachers, (2) the rightful opportunities of pupils to acquire desired knowledge, and (3) the power of parents to determine the education of their children.

The precedential impact of this case is evidenced by the frequency to which it is referred in subsequent cases reported in this publication—especially those involving the issue of parental versus state authority over the pupil.

State legislatures may profit from the guideline laid down in *Meyer* v. *Nebraska.* Despite desirable and beneficial ends, they cannot be accomplished by legislation which is in conflict with provisions of the Federal Constitution.

Chapter 3

PUBLIC SCHOOL ATTENDANCE
REQUIREMENT

(held unconstitutional)

Pierce v. *Society of Sisters* (Ore.),
268 U.S. 510, 45 S. Ct. 571 (1925)

The Issue. The question in this case was whether
or not a state statute was valid which *required*
children to attend *public* schools rather than *private*
schools. The trial court reduced the issue to the
following brief query: "Has the state, through its
legislative functions, the power, under the guise of
police regulation, to deprive parochial and private
school organizations of the liberty and right to carry
on their schools for teaching in the grammar
grades?" (296 F. at 936)

Background. The litigation in this case grew out of
an Oregon law designed to prohibit private
elementary schools. The contested act stipulated
that:

> Any parent, guardian, or other person in
> the state of Oregon, having control or
> charge or custody of a child under the age of
> sixteen years and of the age of eight years or
> over at the commencement of a term of
> public school of the district in which said
> child resides, who shall fail or neglect or
> refuse to send such child to a public school

for the period of time a public school shall
be held during the current year in said
district, shall be guilty of a misdemeanor
and each day's failure to send such child to a
public school shall constitute a separate
offense. . . . (*Id.* at 930)

Action to bar enforcement of the act was initiated
by two Oregon corporations owning and conducting
schools—namely, (1) Society of the Holy Names of
Jesus and Mary, and (2) Hill Military Academy.
Among the powers assumed by the Sisters' Society is
"the care of orphans and the education and
instruction of youth, and to establish and maintain
academies or schools for the care and education of
youth in the cities and towns of the state of Oregon"
and among those assumed by the Academy, "to
conduct a military academy and school." (*Id.* at 930)

District Court Decision. Before a 3-judge federal
district court, in March of 1924, plaintiffs sought to
have the act declared void because it was "violative of
section 1 of the Fourteenth Amendment of the
Constitution, in that it trenches upon their privileges
and immunities as citizens of the United States; that
it deprives them of life, liberty, and property without
due process of law, and the equal protection of the
laws. . . ." (*Id.* at 931)

The arguments presented by the plaintiff were
convincing to the district court, as indicated by its
concluding statement:

So it is here, in our opinion, the state,
acting in its legislative capacity, has, in the
means adopted, exceeded the limitations of

its power—its purpose being to take utterly away from complainants their constitutional right and privilege to teach in the grammar grades—and has and will deprive them of their property without due process of law. (*Id.* at 938)

U. S. Supreme Court Decision. Before rendering a decision, the United States Supreme Court entertained lengthy arguments, pro and con, with respect to the validity of the contested Oregon law.

Among the arguments *challenging the constitutionality* of the law were the following:

... the true purpose of the act, as well as its plain and intended practical effect, was the destruction of private primary, preparatory and parochial schools; for they certainly could not survive the denial of the right of parents to have their children thus educated in the primary grades. Such drastic and extraordinary legislation is a portentous innovation in America. (268 U.S. 510, at 514, 1925)
The legislation before the court manifestly carries within itself a threat, not merely to the private elementary and preparatory schools which it now practically proscribes, but to every private or religious college or university in the land. The statute in suit is so unusual and extraordinary that it must arouse misgivings in the judicial mind upon even the slightest reflection." (*Id.* at 515)
The statute abridges the freedom of four classes closely interrelated: (1) the freedom of the private and parochial schools, (2) the

freedom of teachers engaged in those schools, (3) the freedom of parents and guardians, and (4) the freedom of children. (*Id.* at 515)

The statute in suit trespasses, not only upon the liberty of the parents individually, but upon their liberty collectively as well. ... In whatever light the act in suit be regarded, it must be manifest that, in the end, it embodies the pernicious policy of state monopoly of education. (*Id.* at 519)

Some of the arguments *supporting the constitutionality* of the statute were the following:

Under all governments, even those which are the most free and democratic in their character, the citizen must always owe duties to the State. ... The discretionary powers of a State are broad enough to permit it to decide that compulsory attendance at public schools is a precautionary measure against the moral pestilence of paupers, vagabonds, and possibly convicts. (*Id.* at 524)

The compulsory attendance of all children of school age at the public schools during the relatively short hours during which these schools are in session would not deprive the parents of any just rights. There would remain an abundance of time and opportunity for supplementary instruction either in religion or in the language, history, and traditions of the land of their ancestors. (*Id.* at 525)

The Oregon law does not deny the equal protection of the law. ... The right to the equal protection of the law is not denied when it is apparent that the same law or course of procedure is applicable to every other person in the State under similar circumstances and conditions. (*Id.* at 527)

The discretion of the States in the exercise of their powers is broad enough to justify a State in holding that a compulsory system of public school education will encourage the patriotism of its citizens, and train its younger citizens to become more willing and efficient defenders of the United States in times of public danger. . . . If a State cannot compel certain children to attend the public schools it cannot compel any children to do so. An attempt to do so would be clearly a violation of the "equal protection of the laws" clause of the Fourteenth Amendment. (*Id.* at 528)

After hearing the above arguments from both sides, the United States Supreme Court rendered a unanimous decision, affirming the decision of the trial court that *the law was unconstitutional* because it interfered with rights granted by the Constitution and was not the type of reasonable regulation of private education that lies within the power of the State.

The reasoning of the United States Supreme Court in this case was somewhat similar to that expressed in *Meyer* v. *Nebraska, supra.* The Court's concluding remarks follow:

No question is raised concerning the power of the State reasonably to regulate all schools, to inspect, supervise and examine them, their teachers and pupils; to require that all children of proper age attend some school, that teachers shall be of good moral character and patriotic disposition, that certain studies plainly essential to good citizenship must be taught, and that nothing be taught which is manifestly inimical to the public welfare.

The inevitable practical result of enforcing the Act under consideration would be destructive of appellees' primary schools, and perhaps all other private primary schools for normal children within the State of Oregon. These parties are engaged in a kind of undertaking not inherently harmful, but long regarded as useful and meritorious. Certainly there is nothing in the present records to indicate that they have failed to discharge their obligations to patrons, students or the State. And there are no peculiar circumstances or present emergencies which demand extraordinary measures relative to primary education.

Under the doctrine of *Meyer* v. *Nebraska*, 262 U.S. 390, we think it entirely plain that the Act of 1922 unreasonably interferes with the liberty of parents and guardians to direct the upbringing and education of children under their control. As often heretofore pointed out, rights guaranteed by the Constitution may not be abridged by legislation which has no reasonable relation to some purpose within the competency of the State. The fundamental theory of liberty upon which all governments in this Union repose excludes any general power of the State to standardize its children by forcing them to accept instruction from public teachers only. The child is not the mere creature of the State; those who nurture him and direct his destiny have the right, coupled with the high duty, to recognize and prepare him for additional obligations. (*Id.* at 534, 535)

Significance of the Decision. As in the preceding case, *Meyer* v. *Nebraska*, the decision in *Pierce* v. *Society* has great precedential significance. In virtually all cases pertaining to compulsory school attendance, where the right to meet the requirement by non-public school attendance is involved, reference is made, by the Court, to the decision in *Pierce* v. *Society*.

The right for non-public school instruction in lieu of instruction in the public schools, has even been extended to home instruction. Under certain conditions, home instruction, as well as instruction provided in private or parochial schools, is held legal. Of course the non-public school instruction must conform to the same standards as those imposed upon the public schools. The Court did not contend in this case that attendance at a private elementary school would have been judicially approved had the instruction been short of state requirement for public schools.

If the Court had upheld the Oregon act, it would have undoubtedly spelled the demise of the non-public school systems—not only in Oregon but in all other states as well. Obviously children could not have attended a non-public school and a public school simultaneously. Although those supporting the act contended that "there would remain an abundance of time and opportunity for supplementary instruction" beyond "the period of time a public school shall be held," the resulting schedule for children of elementary-school age would have been unreasonable.

In virtually all cases where legislation is in conflict with "the due process of law" clause of the Fourteenth Amendment, the legislation will be nullified. Legislators would do well to study the opinion of the United States Supreme Court in *Pierce* v. *Society* before proposing an act which would deprive citizens of liberty and property without due process of law and the equal protection of the laws, as guaranteed by the Fourteenth Amendment to the United States Constitution.

Chapter 4

FREE TEXTBOOKS FOR PAROCHIAL PUPILS

(held constitutional)

Cochran v. *Louisiana State Board of Education,*
281 U.S. 370, 50 S. Ct. 335 (1930)

The Issue. The question in this case was whether
or not a Louisiana statute was valid which provided
for the use of *public* funds to supply textbooks, free
of charge, to pupils of *non-public* schools.

Background. The Louisiana Legislature passed an
act in 1928, commonly known as "The Free Text-
Book Act" which authorized the appropriation of
funds necessary for the purchasing of textbooks to be
granted "to the school children of the State."

The State Board of Education construed and
applied the law to include among "the school children
of the State *all* school children, and not necessarily
only those attending the *public* schools." Certain
citizens, however, brought suit to restrain the State
Board of Education from providing the textbooks,
free of charge, to the *non-public* schools. They
contended that public property was being diverted to
private purposes in violation of the Fourteenth
Amendment. In support of their contention they
submitted the following arguments:

The furnishing of text-books free by the

State to school children attending private schools which charge tuition and require the children to furnish their school books, is an aid to such private institutions by furnishing a part of their equipment. If the legislature may not levy a tax for the aid of private schools, it may not indirectly do the same thing. . . .

If the furnishing of text-books free to children attending private schools is not considered an aid to such private schools, but as incidental to the state educational system, then it logically follows that the tuition of the children attending such schools could be paid; their transportation to and from such schools could be provided; the salaries of the instructors could be paid in part or in whole; and finally, the buildings themselves could be erected,—with state funds; all of which, under the reasoning evidenced in the statutes of Louisiana, might be justified on the ground that it is the interest of the State to see that its youth are educated.

If the furnishing of school books to children attending private schools is not to be considered an aid to such private schools but an aid only to the children attending such schools, then the tax levied for such purpose is equally obnoxious to the Federal Constitution because it constitutes a diversion of public property to private individuals without distinction as to need for charity and without any special obligation of the State, charitable or otherwise to such persons. . . .

If the principle upon which there is allowed a diversion of the public school funds for the benefit of private individuals, is sanctioned, then the division of the public school funds may be permitted, so that ultimately those whose children attend private schools, under the simulation of bearing the burden of taxation for the public schools, are paying for the maintenance only of their own private schools. This finally means, in effect, depriving the State of its power to tax (for the support of the public schools) those who support only their private schools — and practically the destruction of one of the free institutions under our republican form of government. (281 U.S. at 371-373)

A trial court refused to issue an injunction, and the Supreme Court of Louisiana affirmed the judgment of the trial court. The case was then appealed to the United States Supreme Court for a final ruling.

U. S. Supreme Court Decision. The Supreme Court of the United States upheld the decision of the Supreme Court of Louisiana sustaining the statute which provided for free textbooks purchased with public funds and distributed to children in nonpublic schools. This decision marked the beginning of the so-called "child benefit theory" which was to be injected into the consideration of subsequent cases.

Chief Justice Hughes delivered the opinion which

was relatively brief. Even in its brevity, the major portion of the opinion was quoted from the opinion of the Louisiana State Court which stated, in part:

> One may scan the acts in vain to ascertain where any money is appropriated for the purchase of school books for the use of any church, private, sectarian or even public school. The appropriations were made for the specific purpose of purchasing school books for the use of the school children of the state, free of cost to them. It was for their benefit and the resulting benefit to the state that the appropriations were made. True, these children attend some school, public or private, the latter, sectarian or non-sectarian, and that the books are to be furnished them for their use, free of cost, whichever they attend. The schools, however, are not the beneficiaries of these appropriations. They obtain nothing from them, nor are they relieved of a single obligation, because of them. The school children and the state alone are the beneficiaries. It is also true that the sectarian schools, which some of the children attend, instruct their pupils in religion, and books are used for that purpose, but one may search diligently the acts, though without result, in an effort to find anything to the effect that it is the purpose of the state to furnish religious books for the use of such children. . . . What the statutes contemplate is that the same books that are furnished children attending public schools shall be furnished children

attending private schools. This is the only
practical way of interpreting and executing
the statutes, and this is what the state
board of education is doing. Among these
books, naturally, none is to be expected,
adapted to religious instruction. (*Id.* at
374-375)

The High Court, being in full agreement with the
viewpoint of the State Supreme Court of Louisiana
concluded its remarks with the following statement:

Viewing the statute as having the effect
thus attributed to it, we cannot doubt that
the taxing power of the State is exerted for a
public purpose. The legislation does not
segregate private schools, of their pupils, as
its beneficiaries or attempt to interfere with
any matters of exclusively private concern.
Its interest is education, broadly; its method
comprehensive. Individual interests are
aided only as the common interest is
safeguarded. (*Id.* at 375)

Significance of the Decision. The decision, in
Cochran, is significant in that it originated the "child
benefit theory"—meaning that public funds may be
allocated to all schools, public or private, providing
the expenditures result in benefits to the pupils.

Many believe the theory can be stretched too far.
In fact proposals are made from time to time to allow
expenditure of public funds for many questionable
purposes which would benefit non-public schools
under the guise of "pupil benefit."

It is rather difficult to conceive of a single school

expenditure which does not, directly or indirectly, benefit the pupil. The school exists for the benefit of the pupil. Therefore the benefits accruing to the school ultimately accrue to the pupil. If carried to extremes it could be argued that since pupils are benefited by having teachers, it is therefore proper to expend public funds for paying salaries to teachers in non-public schools. Or, since pupils are benefited by being housed in buildings, the construction and maintenance for such in non-public schools at public expense is justifiable.

Since legislators and public officials continue to propose the financing of non-public school programs at public expense, the courts are frequently called upon to determine the extent to which this may be done within the limits of the Federal Constitution. The decision in *Cochran* has stimulated incentives as indicated in subsequent court cases. It may be regarded as a landmark decision in that it opened the door to "parochiaid."

Chapter 5

FLAG-SALUTE REQUIREMENT

(held constitutional)

Minersville School District v. *Gobitis* (Pa.),
310 U.S. 586, 60 S. Ct. 1010 (1940)

The Issue. The issue in this case was whether a
school regulation requiring all children to
participate in the daily flag-salute ceremony in the
public classroom was in violation of the First
Amendment's Free Exercise Clause insofar as
children who had religious scruples against
participating were concerned. In the words of Justice
Frankfurter, the issue was "whether the
requirement of participation in such a ceremony,
exacted from a child who refuses upon sincere
religious grounds, infringes without due process of
law guaranteed by the Fourteenth Amendment."
(310 U.S. at 592-3)

Background. The background of the case is
succinctly described by Justice Frankfurter in the
following passage:

> Lillian Gobitis, aged twelve, and her
> brother William, aged ten, were expelled
> from the public schools of Minersville,
> Pennsylvania, for refusing to salute the
> national flag as part of a daily school
> exercise. The local Board of Education
> required both teacher and pupils to
> participate in this ceremony. The ceremony
> is a familiar one. The right hand is placed on

the breast and the following pledge recited in unison: "I pledge allegiance to my flag, and to the Republic for which it stands; one nation indivisible, with liberty and justice for all." While the words are spoken, teachers and pupils extend their right hands in salute to the flag. The Gobitis family are affiliated with the Jehovah's Witnesses, for whom the Bible as the Word of God is the supreme authority. The children had been brought up conscientiously to believe that such a gesture of respect for the flag was forbidden by command of Scripture.

The Gobitis children were of an age for which Pennsylvania makes school attendance compulsory. Thus they were denied a free education, and their parents had to put them in private schools. To be relieved of the financial burden thereby entailed, their father, on behalf of the children and in his own behalf, brought this suit. He sought to enjoin the authorities from continuing to exact participation in the flag-salute ceremony as a condition of his children's attendance at the Minersville school.

On May 3, 1937, counsel for Gobitis filed a bill of complaint in the United States District Court, denouncing the Minersville regulation and the expulsion thereunder as violative of the Eighth and Fourteenth Amendments and requesting an injunction against their continued enforcement against the Gobitis children.

From then on, for several years, first in the District Court and later in the Circuit Court of Appeals, the case was marked with much bickering, confusion, conflicting testimony, and presentation of lengthy briefs. The United States Supreme Court gave the matter full consideration and finally, on March 4, 1940, granted a *writ of certiorari*.

U. S. Supreme Court Decision. In brief, the *United States Supreme Court upheld the Minersville School District regulation that students should salute the American flag as a condition for school attendance.*

Before arriving at that decision, however, the Court heard arguments, pro and con, regarding validity of the school regulation. Among arguments *supporting the regulation* were the following:

> The refusal of the children to salute the national flag at school exercises because they believed that to do so would violate the written law of Almighty God as contained in the Bible was not founded on a religious belief.
>
> The act of saluting the flag has no bearing on what a pupil may think of his Creator. Nor is a pupil required to exhibit his religious sentiments in a particular "form of worship" when saluting the flag, because the ceremony is not, by any stretch of the imagination, a "form of worship." Like the study of history or civics or the doing of any other act which might make a pupil more patriotic as well as teach him or her "loyalty to the State and National Government," the salute has no religious implications. . . . The commandments of Jehovah, as set forth in the Bible, do not prohibit the saluting of a national flag but on the contrary approve of that practice.
>
> The act of saluting the flag is only one of

the many ways in which a citizen may evidence his respect for the Government. The same respect is shown the American flag when it passes in a parade; yet that is not a religious rite.

Though members of Jehovah's Witnesses endeavor to extend religious implications to a ceremony purely patriotic in design, they do not accord to others the religious freedom which they demand for themselves, claiming that there is no limit to which they may go when they think they are worshipping God. . . .

The act of saluting the flag does not prevent a pupil, no matter what his religious belief may be, from acknowledging the spiritual sovereignty of Almighty God by rendering to God the things which are God's. . . . (*Id.* at 587-8)

Arguments *against the regulation* were enunciated as follows:

The rule compelling respondents to participate in the ceremony of saluting the flag and the act of its School Board in expelling them because they refrained, violate their rights guaranteed by . . . the Fourteenth Amendment of the Constitution of the United States.

The vital question is: Shall man be free to exercise his conscientious belief in God and his obedience to the law of Almighty God, or shall man be compelled to obey the law of the State, which law, as the creature, conscientiously believes, is in direct conflict with the laws of Almighty God?

This Court has repeatedly held that the

individual alone is privileged to determine
what he shall or shall not believe. The law,
therefore, does not attempt to settle
differences by creeds and confessions, or to
say that any point or doctrine is too absurd
to be believed. . . .

Will any court attempt to say that
respondents mistakingly believe what is set
forth in the twentieth chapter of Exodus in
the Bible? The belief of the respondents is
not based on conjecture or myth.
Respondent's belief is based strictly on the
Bible. . . .

The saluting of the flag of any earthly
government by a person who has
covenanted to do the will of God is a form of
religion and constitutes idolatry.

To expel children from school and deny
them the opportunity of an education
because they refuse to violate their
conscience, is wrong and is cruel and
unusual punishment. . . .

The rule certainly abridges the privilege
of the respondents and deprives them of
liberty and property without due process of
law. (*Id.* at 589-90)

Justice Frankfurter, who expressed trepidation in
tackling the case, delivered the majority opinion of
the Court in these words:

A grave responsibility confronts this
Court whenever in course of litigation it
must reconcile the conflicting claims of
liberty and authority. But when the liberty
invoked is liberty of conscience, and the
authority is authority to safeguard the
nation's fellowship, judicial conscience is

put to its severest test. Of such a nature is
the present controversy. (*Id.* at 591)

In support of its decision, the Court stressed
educational aspects of the flag-salute requirement in
the following terms:

We are dealing here with the formative
period in the development of citizenship.
Great diversity of psychological and ethical
opinion exists among us concerning the best
way to train children for their place in
society. Because of these differences and
because of reluctance to permit a single,
iron-clad system of education to be imposed
upon a nation compounded of so many
strains, we have held that, even though
public education is one of our most
cherished democratic institutions, the Bill
of Rights bars a state from compelling all
children to attend the public schools. But it
is a very different thing for this Court to
exercise censorship over the conviction of
legislatures that a particular program or
exercise will best promote in the minds of
children who attend the common schools an
attachment to the institutions of their
country. (*Id.* at 598-99)

The preciousness of the family relation,
the authority and independence which give
dignity to parenthood, indeed the enjoyment
of all freedom, presuppose the kind of
ordered society which is summarized by our
flag. A society which is dedicated to the
preservation of these ultimate values of
civilization may in self-protection utilize the
educational process for inculcating those
almost unconscious feelings which bind men

together in a comprehending loyalty, whatever may be their lesser differences and difficulties. . . . (*Id.* at 600)

In his strong dissent, Justice Stone emphasized that even though the state may exercise considerable control over pupils, that control is limited where it interferes with civil liberties guaranteed by the Constitution. He states, in part:

> The guaranties of civil liberty are but guaranties of freedom of the human mind and spirit and of reasonable freedom and opportunity to express them. They presuppose the right of the individual to hold such opinions as he will and to give them reasonably free expression, and his freedom, and that of the state as well, to teach and persuade others by the communication of ideas. The very essence of the liberty which they guarantee in the freedom of the individual from compulsion as to what he shall think and what he shall say, at least where the compulsion is to bear false witness to his religion. If these guaranties are to have any meaning they must, I think, be deemed to withhold from the state any authority to compel belief or the expression of it where that expression violates religious convictions, whatever may be the legislative view of the desirability of such compulsion. (*Id.* at 604)
>
> ... The Constitution may well elicit expressions of loyalty to it and to the government which it created, but it does not command such expressions or otherwise give any indication that compulsory

expressions of loyalty play any such part in our scheme of government as to override the constitutional protection of freedom of speech and religion. And while such expressions of loyalty, when voluntarily given, may promote national unity, it is quite another matter to say that their compulsory expression by children in violation of their own and their parents' religious convictions can be regarded as playing so important a part in our national unity as to leave school boards free to exact it despite the constitutional guarantee of freedom of religion. The very terms of the Bill of Rights preclude, it seems to me, any reconciliation of such compulsions with the constitutional guaranties by a legislative declaration that they are more important to the public welfare than the Bill of Rights. (*Id.* at 605)

The Constitution expresses more than the conviction of the people that democratic processes must be preserved at all costs. It is also an expression of faith and a command that freedom of mind and spirit must be preserved, which government must obey, if it is to adhere to that justice and moderation without which no free government can exist. For this reason it would seem that legislation which operates to repress the religious freedom of small minorities, which is admittedly within the scope of the protection of the Bill of Rights, must at least be subject to the same judicial scrutiny as legislation which we have recently held to infringe the constitutional liberty of religious and racial minorities.

With such scrutiny, I cannot say that the

inconveniences which may attend some sensible adjustment of school discipline in order that the religious convictions of these children may be spared, presents a problem so momentous or pressing as to outweigh the freedom from compulsory violation of religious faith which has been thought worthy of constitutional protection. (*Id.* at 606-7)

Significance of the Decision. The decision in *Minersville* v. *Gobitis* is significant, but academic as far as finalizing a legal precedent is concerned. From the very beginning of litigation there was evidence that a judicial opinion upholding the flag-salute requirement was doomed to a judicial overturn.

As has been indicated there was much logic and merit in the arguments of those who supported the flag-salute requirement as well as the arguments of those who were opposed to it. The Court was compelled to make a delicate decision as to whether or not the desire for a patriotic gesture of saluting the flag outweighed the religious freedom expressed in the Constitution. In this case the balance of support favored the arguments supporting the requirement.

Despite the immediate effect a Supreme Court decision has upon a litigated issue, the eventual results may be more apparent in the dissenting opinions than in the majority opinion. The very next case to which reference will be made confirms this contention. In fact, the comments of Justice Stone, in his strong dissent in *Gobitis*, are strikingly similar to those expressed in the majority opinion in the following flag-salute case to be reported.

Chapter 6

FLAG-SALUTE REQUIREMENT

(held unconstitutional)

West Virginia State Board of Education
v. *Barnette,* 319 U.S. 624, 63 S. Ct.
1178 (1943)

The Issue. The issue in this case was quite similar
to that involved in the preceding case (*Gobitis*) in
that it questioned the validity of a requirement for
children to salute the American flag who claimed
religious scruples against doing so. One difference is
that, in the *Gobitis* case, the validity of a school-
district requirement was challenged, whereas, in this
case *(Barnette),* the challenge had to do with a state-
wide requirement.

Background. Proceedings of the *Gobitis* case
constitute the immediate background for this case.
Before *Gobitis,* however, the flag-salute issue had
been litigated in more than twenty states with
conflicting judicial opinions rendered.

The *Gobitis* decision was destined to be reversed as
soon as it was given. Immediate opposition to the
decision was expressed in newspapers, educational
journals, law journals and law reviews. Moreover,
various groups such as the American Legion, the
American Civil Liberties Union, the American Bar
Association and even the United States Department
of Justice voiced their opposition to the decision
which had upheld the flag-salute requirement.

Moreover, some of the Justices who provided the majority opinion in *Gobitis*, admitted they were having a change of heart in their opinions. And, of course, the forceful dissent of Justice Stone in *Gobitis* was extremely influential in reopening the issue.

The Jehovah's Witnesses took advantage of all the outside support for their opposition to the required flag salute when the West Virginia state legislature "amended its statutes to require all schools therein to conduct courses of instruction in history, civics, and the Constitution of the United States and of the State for the purpose of teaching, fostering and perpetuating the ideals, principles and spirit of Americanism, and increasing the knowledge of the organization and machinery of the government." (319 U.S. at 625)

In accordance with the statutes, the West Virginia State Board of Education adopted a regulation that the salute to the flag become "a regular part of the program of activities in the public schools," that all teachers and pupils "shall be required to participate in the salute honoring the Nation represented by the Flag; provided, however, that refusal to salute the Flag be regarded as an act of insubordination, and shall be dealt with accordingly." (*Id.* at 626)

"Appellees, citizens of the United States and of West Virginia, brought suit in the United States District Court for themselves and others similarly situated asking its injunction to restrain enforcement of these laws and regulations against Jehovah's Witnesses." (*Id.* at 629) The position of the

Jehovah's Witnesses was supported in the three-judge District Court, from whence it was carried to the United States Supreme Court for a final ruling.

U. S. Supreme Court Decision. On June 14, 1943, the United States Supreme Court *upheld the District Court's ruling that the State Board rule requiring all students to salute the flag and recite the pledge of allegiance thereto as a condition of school attendance violated the First Amendment to the Federal Constitution which guarantees the exercise of freedom of religion.*

The majority opinion was written by Justice Jackson and concurred in by Justices Stone, Black, Douglas, Murphy and Rutledge. Justices Roberts and Reed dissented mildly, but Justice Frankfurter wrote an extensive and blistering dissenting opinion which exceeded in length the entire majority opinion plus the concurring opinions.

Noteworthy, in the majority opinion, are the concluding remarks written by Justice Jackson:

> National unity as an end which officials may foster by persuasion and example is not in question. The problem is whether under our Constitution compulsion as here employed is a permissible means for its achievement.
>
> Struggles to coerce uniformity of sentiment in support of some end thought essential to their time and country have been waged by many good as well as evil men. Nationalism is a relatively recent phenomenon but at other times and places the ends have been racial or territorial

security, support of a dynasty or regime, and particular plans for saving souls. As first and moderate methods to attain unity have failed, those bent on its accomplishment must resort to ever-increasing severity. As governmental pressure toward unity becomes greater, so strife becomes more bitter as to whose unity it shall be. Probably no deeper division of our people could proceed from any provocation than from finding it necessary to choose what doctrine and whose program public officials shall compel youth to unite in embracing. Ultimate futility of such attempts to compel coherence is the lesson of every such effort from the Roman drive to stamp out Christianity as a disturber of its pagan unity, the Inquisition, as a means to religious and dynastic unity, the Siberian exiles as a means to Russian unity, down to the fast failing efforts of our present totalitarian enemies. Those who begin coercive elimination of dissent soon find themselves exterminating dissenters. Compulsory unification of opinion achieves only the unanimity of the graveyard.

It seems trite but necessary to say that the First Amendment to our Constitution was designed to avoid these ends by avoiding these beginnings. There is no mysticism in the American concept of the State of the nature or origin of its authority. We set up government by consent of the governed, and the Bill of Rights denies those in power any legal opportunity to coerce that consent. Authority here is to be controlled by public opinion, not public opinion by authority.

The case is made difficult not because the principles of its decision are obscure but because the flag involved is our own. Nevertheless, we apply the limitations of the Constitution with no fear that freedom to be intellectually and spiritually diverse or even contrary will disintegrate the social organization. To believe that patriotism will not flourish if patriotic ceremonies are voluntary and spontaneous instead of a compulsory routine is to make an unflattering estimate of the appeal of our institutions to free minds. We can have intellectual individualism and the rich cultural diversities that we owe to exceptional minds only at the price of occasional eccentricity and abnormal attitudes. When they are so harmless to others or to the State as those we deal with here, the price is not too great. But freedom to differ is not limited to things that do not matter much. That would be a mere shadow of freedom. The test of its substance is the right to differ as to things that touch the heart of the existing order.

If there is any fixed star in our constellation, it is that no official, high or petty, can prescribe what shall be orthodox in politics, nationalism, religion, or other matters of opinion or force citizens to confess by word or act their faith therein. If there are any circumstances which permit an exemption, they do not now occur to us.

We think the action of the local authorities in compelling the flag salute and pledge transcends constitutional limitations on their power and invades the sphere of intellect and spirit which it is the purpose of the First Amendment to our Constitution to reserve from all official control. (*Id.* at 640-42)

Justice Frankfurter was just as forceful in stating his dissent in this case (*Barnette*) as he was in speaking for the majority in the preceding case (*Gobitis*). Several brief excerpts from his lengthy dissenting opinion follow:

> Parents have the privilege of choosing which schools they wish their children to attend. And the question here is whether the state may make certain requirements that seem to it desirable or important for the proper education of those future citizens who go to schools maintained by the states, or whether the pupils in those schools may be relieved from those requirements if they run counter to the consciences of their parents. Not only have parents the right to send children to schools of their own choosing but the state has no right to bring such schools "under a strict governmental control" or give "affirmative direction concerning the intimate and essential details of such schools, entrust their control to public officers, and deny both owners and patrons reasonable choice and discretion in respect of teachers, curriculum and textbooks." Why should not the state likewise have constitutional power to make reasonable provisions for the proper instruction of children in schools maintained by it?
>
> We are told that a flag salute is a doubtful substitute for adequate understanding of our institutions. The states that require

such a school exercise do not have to justify
it as the only means for promoting good
citizenship in children, but merely as one of
diverse means for accomplishing a worthy
end. We may deem it a foolish measure, but
the point is that this Court is not the organ
of government to resolve doubts as to
whether it will fulfill its purpose. Only if
there be no doubt that any reasonable mind
could entertain can we deny to the states the
right to resolve doubts their way and not
ours.

That which to the majority may seem
essential for the welfare of the state may
offend the consciences of a minority. But, so
long as no inroads are made upon the actual
exercise of religion by the minority, to deny
the political power of the majority to enact
laws concerned with civil matters, simply
because they may offend the consciences of
a minority, really means that the
consciences of a minority are more sacred
and more enshrined in the Constitution
than the consciences of a majority. (*Id.* at
661-62)

The flag salute exercise has no kinship
whatever to the oath tests so odious in
history. For the oath test was one of the
instruments for suppressing heretical
beliefs. Saluting the flag suppresses no
belief nor curbs it. Children and their
parents may believe what they please, avow
their belief and practice it. It is not even
remotely suggested that the requirement
for saluting the flag involves the slightest
restriction against the fullest opportunity
on the part both of the children and of their
parents to disavow as publicly as they

choose to do so the meaning that others attach to the gesture of salute. All channels of affirmative free expression are open to both children and parents. Had we before us any act of the state putting the slightest curbs upon free expression, I should not lag behind any member of this Court in striking down such an invasion of the right to freedom of thought and freedom of speech protected by the Constitution. (*Id.* at 663-64)

Significance of the Decision. This is another decision in which it has been ruled that, despite the desirability of a regulation imposed upon students, the regulation is illegal if in conflict with liberties guaranteed by the Constitution. The alleged civic achievements and desirability of a school regulation, such as the flag-salute exercise, must give way to constitutional guarantees.

Despite the High Court's ruling in *Gobitis*, upholding the flag-salute requirement, the opposite ruling in *Barnette*, voiding the requirement, is evidence that even the Supreme Court can be swayed by strong public opposition. This fact may cause speculation that the growing intense opposition to the decisions in the school prayer case and the pupil busing case—to be reported later in this publication—may eventually cause a judicial turnover.

Slight deviations in the circumstances do not alter the 1943 ruling in *Barnette*. For example, in 1969, it was held in a federal court case (*Frain* v. *Baron*, 307 F. Supp. 27, 1969) that a student could not be excluded from the classrooms during the pledge of allegiance merely "for reasons of conscience to participate in Pledge in any different way from those who participate." The Court stated: "The student is free to select his form of expression, so long as it does not materially infringe the rights of other students or disrupt school activities." (*Id.* at 32)

Similarly, in a Florida case (*Banks* v. *Board of Public Instruction of Dade County*, 314 F. Supp. 285, 1970), a United States District Court ruled in favor of a student who was suspended from school as a result of his refusal to stand during the pledge of allegiance. The Court stated: "The right to differ and express one's opinions, to fully vent his First Amendment rights, even to the extent of exhibiting disrespect for our flag and country by refusing to stand and participate in the pledge of allegiance, cannot be suppressed by the imposition of suspension." (*Id.* at 296)

Even teachers, as well as students, need not obey a statutory flag-salute requirement. For example, in a Maryland case (*State* v. *Lundquist*, 278 A.2d 263, 1971) it was revealed that a social science teacher "claimed that he would refuse to engage in a mandatory flag salute ceremony, not for religious reasons, but because he could not in good conscience force patriotism upon his classes." After consideration of the issues raised in this case and preceding cases, in which provisions of the First and Fourteenth Amendments were involved, the Court of Appeals of Maryland concluded that the salute requirement and punishment provision of the Maryland Law "are unconstitutional and void."

The judicial rulings expressed in the above-mentioned cases give evidence that the legal principle in *Barnette* is now quite firmly stabilized.

Chapter 7

FREE TRANSPORTATION FOR PAROCHIAL PUPILS

(held constitutional)

Everson v. Board of Education (N.J.), 330 U.S. 1, 67 S. Ct. 504 (1947)

The Issue. The issue involved in this case concerned the validity of a New Jersey statute to provide free transportation for children attending parochial schools.

Background. The case grew out of a contested statute (New Jersey Laws, 1941, c. 191, p. 581) which reads as follows:

> Whenever in any district there are children living remote from any schoolhouse, the board of education of the district may make rules and contracts for the transportation of such children to and from school, including the transportation of school children to and from school other than a public school, except such school as is operated for profit in whole or in part. (330 U.S. at 3)

By virtue of the statutory provision, reimbursement was ordered to a township school board to parents whose children had been transported to (Catholic) parochial schools. As a consequence, Everson, a taxpayer of the district challenged the legality of the board's action and the constitutionality of the statute which prompted it.

In a suit by a taxpayer, the New Jersey Supreme Court held that the state legislature was without power under the state constitution to authorize reimbursement to parents of bus fares paid for transporting their children to schools other than public schools. . . . The New Jersey Court of Errors and Appeals reversed, holding that neither the statute nor a resolution passed pursuant to it violated the state constitution or the provisions of the Federal Constitution in issue. (*Id.* at 2)

On appeal of the federal question, the case then went to the United States Supreme Court for final settlement.

U. S. Supreme Court Decision. In its five to four decision on February 10, 1947, the United States Supreme Court *sustained the right of local school authorities to provide free transportation for pupils attending the parochial schools in accordance with the New Jersey statute.*

Justice Black delivered the majority opinion of the Court. Selected excerpts from the sixteen-page opinion follow:

The only contention here is that the state statute and the resolution, insofar as they authorized reimbursement to parents of children attending parochial schools, violate the Federal Constitution in these two respects, which to some extent overlap. *First.* They authorize the State to take by taxation the private property of some and bestow it upon others, to be used for their own private purposes. This, it is alleged, violates the due process clause of the Fourteenth Amendment. *Second.* The statute and the resolution forced inhabitants to pay taxes to help support and maintain schools that are dedicated to, and which regularly teach, the Catholic Faith. This is alleged to be a use of state power to support church schools contrary to the prohibition of the First Amendment which the Fourteenth Amendment made applicable to the states. (*Id.* at 5)

Disregarding the above allegations, the Court tated:

It is much too late to argue that legislation intended to facilitate the opportunity of children to get a secular education serves no public purpose. . . . The same thing is no less true of legislation to reimburse needy parents, or all parents, for payment of the fares of their children so that they can ride in public busses to and from schools rather than run the risks of traffic and other hazards incident to walking or "hitchhiking. . . ." Nor does it follow that a law has a private rather than a public purpose because it provides that tax-raised funds will be paid to reimburse individuals on account of money spent by them in a way which furthers a public program. . . . Subsidies and loans to individuals as farmers and home-owners, and to privately owned transportation systems, as well as many other kinds of

> businesses, have been commonplace
> practices in our state and national history.
> (*Id.* at 7)

After giving cognizance to the fact that neither a
state nor the Federal Government can (1) set up a
church; (2) pass laws which aid one religion over
another; or (3) tax in any amount, large or small, to
support any religious activities or institutions to
teach or practice religion, the Court countered by
stating: "We must consider the New Jersey statute in
accordance with the foregoing limitations imposed
by the First Amendment. But we must not strike
that state statute down if it is within the State's
constitutional power even though it approaches the
verge of that power." (*Id.* at 16)

The concluding remarks of the majority opinion
are stated in the following passage:

> Measured by these standards, we cannot
> say that the First Amendment prohibits
> New Jersey from spending tax-raised funds
> to pay the bus fares of parochial school
> pupils as part of a general program under
> which it pays the fares of pupils attending
> public and other schools. It is undoubtedly
> true that children are helped to get to
> church schools. There is even a possibility
> that some of the children might not be sent
> to the church schools if the parents were
> compelled to pay their children's bus fares
> out of their own pockets when trans-
> portation to a public school would have
> been paid for by the State. The same
> possibility exists where the state requires a
> local transit company to provide reduced

fares to school children including those attending parochial schools, or where a municipality owned transportation system undertakes to carry all school children free of charge. Moreover, state-paid policemen, detached to protect children going to and from church schools from the very real hazards of traffic, would serve much the same purpose and accomplish much the same result as state provisions intended to guarantee free transportation of a kind which the state deems to be best for the school children's welfare. And parents might refuse to risk their children to the serious danger of traffic accidents going to and from parochial schools, the approaches to which were not protected by policemen. Similarly, parents might be reluctant to permit their children to attend schools which the state had cut off from such general government services as ordinary police and fire protection, connections for sewage disposal, public highways and sidewalks. Of course, cutting off church schools from these services, so separate and so indisputably marked off from the religious functions, would make it far more difficult for the schools to operate. But such is obviously the purpose of the First Amendment. That Amendment requires the state to be the neutral in its relation with groups of religious believers and non-believers; it does not require the state to be their adversary. State power is no more to be used so as to handicap religions than it is to favor them.

This Court has said that parents may, in

the discharge of their duty under state compulsory education laws, send their children to a religious rather than a public school if the school meets the secular educational requirements which the state has power to impose. It appears that these parochial schools meet New Jersey's requirements. The State contributes no money to the schools. It does not support them. Its legislation, as applied, does no more than provide a general program to help parents get their children, regardless of their religion, safely and expeditiously to and from accredited schools.

The First Amendment has erected a wall between church and state. That wall must be kept high and impregnable. We could not approve the slightest breach. New Jersey has not breached it here.

Affirmed. (Id. at 17-18)

Dissenting Opinions. In a five to four decision rather forceful dissents may be anticipated. Such is the case as illustrated by the dissent of Justice Jackson, who was joined by Justice Frankfurter. He stated in part:

I find myself, contrary to first impressions, unable to join this decision. I have a sympathy, though it is not idealogical, with Catholic citizens who are compelled by law to pay taxes for public schools, and also feel constrained by conscience and discipline to support other schools for their own children. Such relief to them as this case involves is not in itself a serious burden to taxpayers and I had assumed it to be as little serious in principle.

Study of this case convinces me otherwise. The Court's opinion marshals every argument in favor of state aid and puts the case in its most favorable light, but much of its reasoning confirms my conclusions that there are no good grounds upon which to support the present legislation. In fact, the undertones of the opinion, advocating complete and uncompromising separation of church from State, seem utterly discordant with its conclusion yielding support to their commingling in educational matters. The case which irresistibly comes to mind or the most fitting precedent is that of Julia who, according to Byron's reports, "whispering I will ne'er consent,—consented." (*Id.* at 18-19)

It is of no importance in this situation whether the beneficiary of this expenditure of tax-raised funds is primarily the parochial school and incidentally the pupil, or whether the aid is directly bestowed on the pupil with indirect benefits to the school. The state cannot maintain a Church and it can no more tax its citizens to furnish free carriage to those who attend a Church. The prohibition against establishment of religion cannot be circumvented by a subsidy, bonus or reimbursement of expense to individuals for receiving religious instruction and indoctrination. (*Id.* at 24)

Justice Rutledge, who wrote at great length (47 pages), prefaced his dissent with the following quotation from a Bill for Establishing Religious Freedom enacted by the General Assembly of Virginia in 1786: "Well aware that Almighty God hath created the mind free; . . . that to compel a man to furnish contributions of money for the propagation of opinions which he disbelieves, is sinful and tyrannical. . . ." Following the quotation he stated:

> I cannot believe that the great author of those words, or the man who made them law, could have joined in this decision. Neither so high nor so impregnable today as yesterday is the wall raised between church and state by Virginia's great statute of religious freedom and the First Amendment, now made applicable to all the states by the Fourteenth. New Jersey's statute sustained in the first, if indeed it is not the second breach to be made by this Court's action. That a third, and a fourth, and still others will be attempted, we may be sure. For just as *Cochran* v. *Board of Education*, 281 U.S. 370, has opened the way by oblique ruling for this decision, so will the two make wider the breach for a third. Thus with time the most solid freedom steadily gives way before continuing corrosive decision. (*Id.* at 29)

In another paragraph, Justice Rutledge stresses the fact that the state's contribution for transportation of parochial pupils is a contribution to the religion:

> New Jersey's action therefore exactly fits the type of exaction and the kind of evil at which Madison and Jefferson struck. Under the test they framed it cannot be said that the cost of transportation is no part of the

cost of education or of the religious instruction given. That it is a substantial and a necessary element is shown most plainly by the continuing and increasing demand for the state to assume it. Nor is there pretense that it relates only to the similar instruction given in religious schools or that any attempt is or could be made toward allocating proportional shares as between the secular and the religious instruction. It is precisely because the instruction is religious and relates to a particular faith, whether one or another, that parents send their children to religious schools under the *Pierce* doctrine. And the very purpose of the state's contribution is to defray the cost of conveying the pupil to the place where he will receive not simply secular, but also and primarily religious, teaching and guidance. (*Id.* at 46)

Justice Rutledge concludes his dissent by writing thusly:

Two great drives are constantly in motion to abridge, in the name of education, the complete division of religion and civil authority which our forefathers made. One is to introduce religious education and observances into the public schools. The other, to obtain public funds for the aid and support of various private religious schools. ... In my opinion both avenues were closed by the Constitution. Neither should be opened by this Court. The matter is not one of quantity, to be measured by the amount of money expended. Now as in Madison's day it is one of principle, to keep separate spheres as the First Amendment drew them; to prevent the first experiment upon our liberties; and to keep the question from becoming entangled in corrosive precedents. We should not be less strict to keep strong and untarnished the one side of the shield of religious freedom than we have been of the other.

The judgment should be reversed. (*Id.* at 63)

Significance of the Decision. The previously cited decision in the textbook case (*Cochran*) has been regarded as the establishment of the child benefit theory, whereby it was held legal to expend public funds for benefits accruing *mainly* to the pupil, even though *indirectly* aiding the parochial school also. The decision in this case (*Everson*) may be regarded as an expansion of the child benefit theory.

The *Cochran* decision, permitting an opening of the door to the public treasury in aid to parochial schools, was destined to encourage a further opening. This was accomplished in *Everson*. It is significant to note, however, that some judicial reluctance to further the child benefit concept and, thereby, breach the wall separating church and state, was beginning to develop. Whereas, the Court was unanimous in allowing the expenditure of public funds to supply textbooks to parochial school pupils, the right to allocate public funds for the transportation of parochial-school pupils was determined by a split five to four decision.

It could be expected that a court decision with such a narrow margin would not settle permanently the

issue of public aid for non-public schools. The strong
and seemingly logical dissenting opinions in *Everson*
are bound to cause public and judicial differences
pertaining to subsequent litigation on the issue.
Excerpts from both the majority opinion and
dissenting opinions of *Everson* are quoted in arguing
later cases where state-school relations are involved.

Chapter 8

RELEASED TIME FOR RELIGIOUS INSTRUCTION

(held unconstitutional)

McCollum v. *Board of Education* (Ill.),
333 U.S. 203, 68 S. Ct. 461 (1948)

The Issue. The issue in this case was whether or not public-school pupils could legally be released from their regular classes to attend sectarian religious instruction during the regular school in public school buildings, under provisions of the "Establishment Clause" of the First Amendment.

Background. A "released-time program" as conducted in the public schools of Champaign, Illinois, was briefly described by the Court in the following terms:

> In 1940 interested members of the Jewish, Roman Catholic, and a few of the Protestant faiths formed a voluntary association called the Champaign Council on Religious Education. They obtained permission from the Board of Education to offer classes in religious instructions to public school pupils in grades four to nine inclusive. Classes were made up of pupils whose parents signed printed cards requesting that their children be permitted to attend; they were held weekly, thirty minutes for the lower grades, forty-five minutes for the higher. The council employed the religious teachers at no expense to the school authorities, but the instructors were subject to the approval

and supervision of the superintendent of
schools. The classes were taught in three
separate religious groups by Protestant
teachers, Catholic priests, and a Jewish
rabbi, although for the past several years
there have apparently been no classes
instructed in the Jewish religion. Classes
were conducted in the regular classrooms of
the school building. Students who did not
choose to take the religious instruction were
not released from public school duties; they
were required to leave their classrooms and
go to some other place in the school building
for pursuit of their secular studies. On the
other hand, students who were released
from secular study for the religious
instructions were required to be present at
the religious classes. Reports of their
presence or absence were made to their
secular teachers. (333 U.S. at 207-9)

The appellant in the case, Vashti McCollum, who
was an avowed atheist began mandamus action
against the Champaign Board of Education in the
Circuit Court of Champaign County, Illinois. Her
asserted interest was that of a resident and taxpayer
of Champaign and a parent whose child was then
enrolled in the Champaign public schools.

Mrs. McCollum charged that the joint public-
school religious-group program violated the First
and Fourteenth Amendments to the United States
Constitution. The Circuit Court dismissed her
petition, and the dismissal was affirmed by the State
Supreme Court, from whence it was appealed to the
United States Supreme Court.

U. S. Supreme Court Decision. The action of the Supreme Court of Illinois was reversed by the United States Supreme Court. In brief, the High Court ruled that *religious instruction in the public school buildings during public-school time as practiced in the Champaign Public Schools, was illegal under the First and Fourteenth Amendments to the Federal Constitution because it amounted to an "establishment of religion."*

Justice Black, who delivered the opinion of the Court stated, in part:

> The foregoing facts, without reference to others that appear in the record, show the use of tax-supported property for religious instruction and the close cooperation between the school authorities and the religious council in promoting religious education. The operation of the State's compulsory education system thus assists and is integrated with the program of religious instruction carried on by separate religious sects. Pupils compelled by law to go to school for secular education are released in part from their legal duty upon the condition that they attend the religious classes. This is beyond all question a utilization of the tax-established and tax-supported public school system to aid religious groups to spread their faith. And it falls squarely under the ban of the First Amendment. (*Id.* at 209-10)

Justice Frankfurter, in a concurring opinion, placed stress upon the "separation of State and

Church" principle, as indicated in the following passages:

> Religious education so conducted on school time and property is patently woven into the working scheme of the school. The Champaign arrangement thus presents powerful elements of inherent pressure by the school system in the interest of religious sects. The fact that this power has not been used to discriminate is beside the point. Separation is a requirement to abstain from fusing functions of Government and of religious sects, not merely to treat them all equally. That a child is offered an alternative may reduce the constraint; it does not eliminate the operation of influence by the school in matters sacred to conscience and outside the school's domain. The law of imitation operates, and non-conformity is not an outstanding characteristic of children. The result is an obvious pressure upon children to attend. Again, while the Champaign school population represents only a fraction of the more than two hundred and fifty sects of the nation, not even all the practicing sects in Champaign are willing or able to provide religious instruction. The children belonging to these non-participating sects will thus have inculcated in them a feeling of separation when the school should be the training ground for habits of community, or they will have religious instruction in a faith which is not that of their parents. As a result, the public school system of Champaign actively furthers inculcation in

the religious tenets of some faith. and in the process sharpens the consciousness of religious differences at least among some of the children committed to its care. These are consequences not amenable to statistics. But they are precisely the consequences against which the Constitution was directed when it prohibited the Government common to all from becoming embroiled, however innocently, in the destructive religious conflicts of which the history of even this country records some dark pages. (*Id.* at 227-28)

. . . We find that the basic Constitutional principle of absolute Separation was violated when the State of Illinois, speaking through its Supreme Court, sustained the school authorities of Champaign in sponsoring and effectively furthering religious beliefs by its educational arrangement.

Separation means separation, not something less. Jefferson's metaphor in describing the relation between Church and State speaks of a "wall of separation" not a fine line easily overstepped. The public school is at once the symbol of our democracy and the most pervasive means for promoting our common destiny. In no activity of the State is it more vital to keep out divisive forces than in its schools, to avoid confusing, not to say fusing, what the Constitution sought to keep strictly apart. . . . (*Id.* at 231)

In another concurring opinion, Justice Jackson made the following observation and warning:

> To me, the sweep and detail of these complaints is a danger signal which warns of the kind of local controversy we will be required to arbitrate if we do not place appropriate limitation on our decision and exact strict compliance with jurisdictional requirements. Authorities list 256 separate and substantial religious bodies to exist in the continental United States. Each of them, through the suit of some discontented but unpenalized and untaxed representative, has as good a right as this plaintiff to demand that the courts compel the schools to sift out of their teaching everything inconsistent with its doctrines. If we are to eliminate everything that is objectionable to any of these warring sects or inconsistent with any of their doctrines, we will leave public education in shreds. Nothing but educational confusion and a discrediting of the public school system can result from subjecting it to constant law suits. (*Id.* at 235)

Justice Reed, the lone dissenter to the Court's opinion, indicated his opposition as indicated by a couple of excerpts from his 19-page report:

> I find it difficult to extract from the opinions any conclusion as to what it is in the Champaign plan that is unconstitutional. Is it the use of school buildings for religious instruction; the release of pupils by the schools for religious instruction during school hours; the so-

called assistance by teachers in handing out the request cards to pupils; in keeping lists of them for release and records of their attendance; or the action of the principals in arranging an opportunity for the classes and the appearance of the Council's instructors? None of the reversing opinions say whether the purpose of the Champaign plan for religious instruction during school hours is unconstitutional or whether it is some ingredient used in or omitted from the formula that makes the plan unconstitutional. (*Id.* at 240)

This Court cannot be too cautious in upsetting practices imbedded in our society by many years of experience. A state is entitled to have great leeway in its legislation when dealing with the important social problems of our population. A definite violation of legislative limits must be established. The Constitution should not be stretched to forbid national customs in the way Courts act. . . . Devotion to the great principle of religious liberty should not lead us into a rigid interpretation of the constitutional guarantee that conflicts with accepted habits of our people. This is an instance where, for me, the history of past practices is determinative of the meaning of a constitutional clause, not a decorous introduction to the study of its text. (*Id.* at 256)

Significance of the Decision. Never before had there been a more forceful and unequivocal denunciation of church-school entanglements than that expressed in the majority opinion of *McCollum.*

State courts, and even the federal courts, had struck down certain practices of religious involvements in the public schools, but usually with some reservation and exceptions. In this case, however, the Court was adamant in abiding strictly by the "separation of the church and state" principle. It left no doubt in its upholding the impregnability of the "wall of separation."

Had the Court decided differently than it did there is no doubt but what numerous conflicts would have risen in the school buildings, not only between school authorities and religious instructors but also, between personnel of the competing religious sects involved. The *McCollum* decision precluded further litigation on the issue under conditions such as those in the Champaign released-time program.

As has been the case in other instances, however, the losing litigants can frequently capitalize on excerpts from the dissenting opinion. It may be noted from the queries raised in Justice Reed's dissent that had certain circumstances been different, the practices in the Champaign program might have been judicially approved. In fact the decision in the next case to be reviewed confirms the possibility.

Chapter 9

RELEASED TIME FOR RELIGIOUS INSTRUCTION

(held constitutional)

Zorach v. *Clauson* (N.Y.), 343 U.S. 306, 72 S. Ct. 679 (1952)

The Issue. The issue here, in *Zorach*, is similar to that in the preceding *McCollum* case in that it has to do with "released time." More specifically, in this case, the question is whether public-school pupils may be released from their religious classes to attend sectarian religious instruction during the regular school hours but *away from* public-school buildings, under provisions of the First Amendment to the United States Constitution.

Background. Under section 3210 of the New York Education Law and the regulations thereunder, New York City:

> permits its public schools to release students during school hours, on written requests of their parents, so that they may leave the school buildings and grounds and go to religious centers for religious instruction or devotional exercises. The same section makes school attendance compulsory; students not released stay in the classrooms; and the churches report to the schools the names of children released from public schools who fail to report for religious instruction. The program involves

neither religious instruction in public schools nor the expenditure of public funds. (343 U.S. at 306)

Zorach and others, being tax payers and residents of New York City, challenged the above law on the grounds that, in essence, it was no different from the one involved in the *McCollum* case, which was declared unconstitutional. They argued that:

> the weight and influence of the school is put behind a program for religious instruction; public school teachers police it, keeping tab on students who are released; the classroom activities come to a halt while the students who are released for religious instruction are on leave; the school is a crutch on which the churches are leaning for support in their religious training; without the cooperation of the schools this "released time" program, like the one in the *McCollum* case, would be futile and ineffective. (*Id.* at 309-10)

The New York Court of Appeals was not convinced by the above argument, and therefore sustained the constitutionality of the New York law. The case was then appealed to the United States Supreme Court.

U. S. Supreme Court Decision. The United States Supreme Court, in a six to three decision upheld the ruling of the New York Court of Appeals in that the *New York law was not unconstitutional,* and that therefore the action of the school board of the City of New York in providing a "released time" program for religious instruction during school hours but away from public school buildings was not in conflict with the First Amendment of the Federal Constitution.

Justice Douglas, who delivered the majority opinion, pointed out that the educational merits of the "released time" program were not involved. He stated, in part:

> The briefs and arguments are replete with data bearing on the merits of this type of "released time" program. Views *pro* and *con* are expressed, based on practical experience with these programs and with their implications. We do not stop to summarize these materials nor to burden the opinion with an analysis of them. For they involve consideration not germane to the narrow constitutional issue presented. They largely concern wisdom of the system, its efficiency from an educational point of view, and the political considerations which have motivated its adoption or rejection in some communities. Those matters are of no concern here, since our problem reduces itself to whether New York by this system has either prohibited the "free exercise" of religion or has made a law "respecting an establishment of religion" within the meaning of the First Amendment. (*Id.* at 310)

The Court added:

> It takes obtuse reasoning to inject any issue of the "free exercise" of religion into the present case. No one is forced to go to the religious classroom and no religious exercise or instruction is brought to the classrooms of the public schools. A student need not take religious instruction. He is left to his own desires as to the manner or time of his religious devotions, if any.

There is a suggestion that the system involves the use of coercion to get public school students into religious classrooms. There is no evidence in the record before us that supports that conclusion. The present record indeed tells us that the school authorities are neutral in this regard and do no more than release students whose parents so request. If in fact coercion were used, if it were established that any one or more teachers were using their office to persuade or force students to take the religious instruction, a wholly different case would be presented. . . . (*Id.* at 310-11)

In continuing its defense for its decision the Court stated:

> . . . we find no constitutional requirement which makes it necessary for government to be hostile to religion and to throw its weight against efforts to widen the effective scope of religious influence. The government must be neutral when it comes to competition between sects. It may not thrust any sect on any person. It may not make a religious observance compulsory. It may not coerce anyone to attend church, to observe a religious holiday, or to take religious instruction. But it can close its doors or suspend its operation as to those who want to repair their religious sanctuary for worship or instruction. No more than this is undertaken here. (*Id.* at 314)

By way of refuting Zorach's contention that the

issues in *McCollum* and *Zorach* were similar, the Court concluded with the following statement:

> ... The problem, like many problems in constitutional law, is one of degree. ...
>
> In the *McCollum* case the classrooms were used for religious instruction and the force of the public school was used to promote that instruction. Here, as we have said, the public schools do no more than accommodate their schedules to a program of outside religious instruction. We follow the *McCollum* case. But we cannot expand it to cover the present released time program unless separation of Church and State means that public institutions can make no adjustments of their schedules to accommodate the religious needs of the people. We cannot read into the Bill of Rights such a philosophy of hostility to religion. (*Id.* at 314-15)

Justices Black, Frankfurter and Jackson delivered separate dissenting opinions. Justice Black indicated the likeness of this case to the *McCollum* case in these words:

> I see no significant difference between the invalid Illinois system and that of New York here sustained. Except for the use of the school buildings in Illinois, there is no difference between the systems which I consider even worthy of mention. In the New York program, as in that of Illinois, the school authorities release some of the children on the condition that they attend to religious classes, get reports on whether

they attend, and hold the other children in the school building until the religious hour is over. As we attempted to make categorically clear, the *McCollum* decision would have been the same if the religious classes had not been held in the school building. (*Id.* at 316)

Justice Frankfurter, in his dissent, made the following comment:

... If every one is free to make what use he will of time wholly unconnected from schooling required by law—those who wish sectarian instruction devoting it to that purpose, those who receive ethical instruction at home, to that, those who study music, to that—then of course there is no conflict with the Fourteenth Amendment.

The pith of the case is that formalized religious instruction is substituted for other school activity which those who do not participate in the released-time program are compelled to attend. The school system is very much in operation during this kind of released time. If its doors are closed, they are closed upon those students who do not attend the religious instruction, in order to keep them within the school. That is the very thing which raises the constitutional issue. It is not met by disregarding it. Failure to discuss this issue does not take it out of the case. (*Id.* at 320-21)

Justice Jackson ended his dissent with the following ridicule:

The day that this country ceases to be free for irreligion it will cease to be free for religion—except for the sect that can win political power. The same epithetical jurisprudence used by the Court today to beat down those who oppose pressuring children into some religion can devise as good epithets tomorrow against those who object to pressuring them into a favored religion. . . the *McCollum* case has passed like a storm in a teapot. The wall which the Court was professing to erect between Church and State has become even more warped and twisted than I expected. Today's judgment will be more interesting to students of psychology and of the judicial processes than to students of constitutional law. (*Id.* at 325)

Significance of the Decision. Although just four years elapsed between the *McCollum* case and the *Zorach* case, there has been no more litigation, at the federal court level, on the issue of released time, during the following two decades. Normally one would suppose that with the judicial approval of released time in the latter case there would be a marked increase in released-time programs throughout the country. Apparently such has not been true. The likely reason is that, in order to have a program judicially approved, it must operate under very restricted conditions. Many parents are not anxious to have their children transferred from school buildings to religious centers for sectarian instruction during the regular school hours. Dual enrolment might be considered a better alternative.

The decision in *Zorach* illustrates that the *amount* of religious influence injected into the public-school program is what perplexes the judiciary and causes split decisions. As one of the justices stated: "The problem, like many problems in constitutional law, is one of degree." Six of the justices believed the religious influence of the New York program was not so excessive as to make it unconstitutional. The three dissenting justices, however, were of the opinion that just the slightest entanglement of church-school relations, as exhibited in the *Zorach* case, was sufficient reason for invalidating the program.

Chapter 10

DISMISSAL OF TEACHERS FOR REFUSAL TO COMPLY WITH OATH REQUIREMENTS

(held constitutional)

Adler v. *Board of Education of City of New York*, 342 U.S. 485, 72 S. Ct. 380 (1952)

The Issue. The issue in *Adler* was whether a Civil Service Law of New York, implemented by the Feinberg Law, makes ineligible for employment in any public schools any member of any organization advocating the overthrow of the Government by force, violence or any unlawful means.

Background. This case had its origin immediately after the enactment of the Feinberg Law of 1949. The legislative frame of mind in enacting the law was vividly depicted in the preamble to the Feinberg Law which reads, in part, as follows:

> The legislature hereby finds and declares that there is common report that members of subversive groups, and particularly of the communist party and certain of its affiliated organizations, have infiltered into public employment in the public schools of the state. . . . The consequence of any such infiltration into the public schools is that subversive propaganda can be disseminated among children of tender years by

those who teach them and to whom the
children look for guidance, authority and
leadership. ... The legislature deplores
the failure heretofore to prevent such infiltration which threatens dangerously
to become a commonplace in our schools.
(New York Education Law, Title V,
Article 61, Sec. 3022)

The actual law then provided that the Board of
Regents, which has charge of the public-school
system of the state, shall after full notice and
hearing, make a listing of organizations which it
finds advocate, advise, teach or embrace the doctrine
that the government should be overthrown by force,
violence, or any other unlawful means. The statute
authorized the Board of Regents to provide, by rule,
that membership in any listed organization, after
notice and hearing "shall constitute prima facie
evidence for disqualification for appointment to or
retention in any office or position in the school
system."

It followed that Adler and several other teachers
were dismissed from their positions by the New York
City Board of Education for their refusal to comply
with the oath requirement involving the Feinberg
Law, whereupon the dismissed teachers appealed to
the Supreme Court of Kings Mountain, with the hope
of having the Feinberg Law declared unconstitutional along with the action of the school
board. The teachers were successful to that point but
then the school board appealed. The Appellate
Division of the Supreme Court reversed the
judgment of the lower court, after which the teacher

appealed again, this time to the Court of Appeals of New York. The Court of Appeals upheld the teachers' dismissal, and then the teachers finally appealed to the highest court in the land.

U. S. Supreme Court Decision. The United States Supreme Court ruled against Adler, thereby sustaining the New York Law and the school board's action in dismissing teachers who violated the anti-subversive law.

Justice Minton, speaking for the majority of the Court, which was divided six to three, stated, in part:

> It is clear that such persons have the right under our law to assemble, speak, think and believe as they will. . . . It is equally clear that they have no right to work for the State in the school system on their own terms. They may work for the school system upon the reasonable terms laid down by the proper authorities of New York. If they do not choose to work on such terms, they are at liberty to retain their beliefs and associations and go elsewhere. Has the State thus deprived them of any right to free speech or assembly? We think not. Such persons are or may be denied, under the statutes in question, the privilege of working for the school system of the State of New York because, first, of their advocacy of the overthrow of the government by force or violence, or, secondly, by unexplained membership in an organization found by the school authorities, after notice and hearing, to teach and advocate the overthrow of the government by force or violence, and known

by such persons to have such purpose. (342 U.S. at 492)

Justice Minton added the following passage which has since been frequently quoted in educational and legal publications dealing with legal rights and restraints of teachers' liberties:

A teacher works in a sensitive area in a schoolroom. There he shapes the attitude of young minds towards the society in which they live. In this, the state has a vital concern. It must preserve the integrity of the schools. That the school authorities have the right and the duty to screen the officials, teachers, and employees as to their fitness to maintain the integrity of the schools as a part of ordered society, cannot be doubted. One's associates, past and present, as well as one's conduct, may properly be considered in determining fitness and loyalty. From time immemorial, one's reputation has been determined in part by the company he keeps. In the employment of officials and teachers of the school system, the state may very properly inquire into the company they keep, and we know of no rule, constitutional or otherwise, that prevents the state, when determining the fitness and loyalty of such persons, from considering the organizations and persons with whom they associate.

If, under the procedure set up in the New York law, a person is found to be unfit and is disqualified from employment in the public school system because of membership in a listed organization, he is not thereby denied the right of free speech and assembly. His freedom of choice between membership in the organization and employment in the school system might be limited, but not his freedom of speech or assembly, except in the remote sense that limitation is inherent in every choice. Certainly such limitation is not one the state may not make in the exercise of its police power to protect the schools from pollution and thereby to defend its own existence. (*Id.* at 493)

In his dissent, Justice Black stated:

... Basically these laws rest on the belief that government should supervise and limit the flow of ideas into the minds of men. The tendency of such governmental policy is to mould people into a common intellectual pattern. Quite a different governmental policy rests on the belief that government should leave the mind and spirit of man absolutely free. Such a governmental policy encourages varied intellectual outlooks in the belief that the best views will prevail. This policy of freedom is in my judgment embodied in the First Amendment and made applicable to the states by the Fourteenth. Because of this policy public officials cannot be constitutionally vested with powers to select the ideas people can think about, censor the public views they can express, or choose the persons or groups people can associate with. Public officials with such powers are not public servants; they are public masters. (*Id.* at 497)

Justice Frankfurter introduced his dissent with the following comment:

> We are asked to pass on a scheme to counteract what are currently called "subversive" influences in the public school system of New York. The scheme is formulated partly in statutes and partly in administrative regulations, but all of it is still an unfinished blueprint. We are asked to adjudicate claims against the constitutionality before the scheme has been put into operation, before the limits it imposes upon free inquiry and association, the scope of scrutiny that it sanctions, and the procedural safeguards that will be found to be implied for its enforcement have been authoritatively defined. I think we should adhere to the teaching of this Court's history to avoid constitutional adjudications on merely abstract or speculative issues and to base them on the concreteness afforded by an actual, present, defined controversy, appropriate for judicial judgment, between adversaries immediately affected by it. In accordance with the settled limits upon our jurisdiction I would dismiss this appeal. (*Id.* at 497-8)

The viewpoint expressed by Douglas, in his dissent, is one which has been increasingly supported by other courts, as well as the general public. Justice Douglas stated, in part:

> I have not been able to accept the recent doctrine that a citizen who enters the public service can be forced to sacrifice his civil rights. I cannot for example find in our

constitutional scheme the power of a state to place its employees in the category of second-class citizens by denying them freedom of thought and expression. The Constitution guarantees freedom of thought and expression to everyone in our society. All are entitled to it; and none needs it more than the teacher.

The public school is in most respects the cradle of our democracy. The increasing role of the public school is seized upon by proponents of the type of legislation represented by New York's Feinberg Law as proof of the importance and need for keeping the school free of "subversive influences." But that is to misconceive the effect of this type of legislation. Indeed the impact of this kind of censorship on the public school system illustrates the high purpose of the First Amendment in freeing speech and thought from censorship. (*Id.* at 508)

The very threat of such a procedure is certain to raise havoc with academic freedom. Youthful indiscretions, mistaken causes, misguided enthusiasm—all long forgotten—become the ghosts of a harrowing present. Any organization committed to a liberal cause, any group organized to revolt against an hysterical trend, any committee launched to sponsor an unpopular program becomes suspect. These are the organizations into which Communists often infiltrate. Their presence infects the whole, even though the project was not conceived in sin. A teacher caught in that mesh is almost certain to stand condemned. Fearing condemnation, she will tend to shrink from any association that stirs controversy. In that manner freedom of expression will be stifled. (*Id.* at 509)

Significance of the Decision. The decision in this case should be viewed in the light of the time at which it was rendered. The chronological record of court cases gives some indication of judicial interpretations of the First Amendment to fit the needs of the times. During normal times the courts interpret the constitutional guarantee of freedom rather rigidly. During a period of great national crisis, however, such as existed during the early fifties, when there was manifest an imminent danger of the overthrow of our government and our Constitution, it was only natural that a more liberal interpretation would come from our judiciary, as well as others.

The decision in *Adler* gives evidence of a liberal interpretation of the First Amendment rights of freedom of speech and thought. That this trend was to be challenged, however, was indicated by the strong statements expressed in dissenting opinions. Viewpoints expressed by Justice Douglas, in his dissent, especially presaged a position to be taken by the United States Supreme Court on a somewhat similar issue nearly two decades later. The *split decision* in cases pertaining to the issue indicate that it has not been permanently resolved.

Chapter 11

SEGREGATION OF THE RACES IN THE PUBLIC SCHOOLS

(held unconstitutional)

Brown v. *Board of Education* (Kan.), 347 U.S.
483, 74 S. Ct. 686 (1954)

The Issue. The issue in this case, as expressed by the Court, was whether "segregation of white and Negro children in the public schools of a State solely on the basis of race, pursuant to state laws permitting or requiring such segregation, denies to Negro children the equal protection of the laws guaranteed by the Fourteenth Amendment—even though the physical facilities and other 'tangible' factors of white and Negro schools may be equal." (347 U.S. at 483)

Background. Related litigation on the issue began in 1896, when a case (*Plessy* v. *Ferguson*), which did not deal directly with a school situation, came before the United States Supreme Court for a settlement. The case concerned the constitutionality of an act of the general assembly of the state of Louisiana passed in 1890, providing for "equal but separate" accommodations for the white and Negro races, by providing two or more passenger coaches for each passenger train.

Plessy, a Negro, violated the act by refusing to leave a coach designated for whites. Upon his arrest, he challenged the constitutionality of the act because it forbade admission solely because of color, which allegedly was violative of the Fourteenth Amendment. The Supreme Court upheld the constitutionality of the state law with the claim that it was necessary to issue absolute equality for both races before the law.

Fortified by the "separate but equal" principle laid down in *Plessy* a number of states provided in their constitutions and statutes for the establishment and operation of segregated schools.

The "separate but equal" principle was not vigorously challenged in the courts for several decades. A climax, however, was approaching as early as 1950 when the United States Supreme Court struck down forced segregation practices in the graduate law schools of Oklahoma and Texas.

The rulings for the university cases motivated litigation for their application to the elementary and secondary school levels. Consequently the *Brown* case was started in 1951 when the parents of Linda Brown, a Negro elementary pupil, challenged a school board's requirement that the girl had to attend a Negro school which was inferior to a white school and further in distance from her home. It was contended that segregation in and of itself causes inferiority and is thus a denial of due process and equal protection.

The United States District Court agreed that segregation in the public schools had a detrimental effect but declined to veer away from the judicially-established "separate but equal" principle laid down in *Plessy*. Consequently the *Brown* case plus similar cases from South Carolina, Virginia, and Delaware went to the United States Supreme Court for a final ruling.

U. S. Supreme Court Decision. On May 17, 1954, one of the most spectacular and significant judicial decisions of the century was handed down, without dissent, by the United States Supreme Court. In essence, the *Court held that segregation of white and Negro children in the public schools solely on the basis of race, denied to Negro children the equal protection of the laws guaranteed by the Fourteenth Amendment and was therefore unconstitutional.*

Chief Justice Warren delivered the unanimous opinion of the Court, the thrust of which is expressed, without embellishment, in the following quotation:

> . . . there are findings below that the Negro and white schools involved have been equalized, or are being equalized, with respect to buildings, curricula, quali- fications and salaries of teachers, and other "tangible" factors. Our decision, therefore, cannot turn on merely a comparison of these tangible factors in the Negro and white schools involved in each of the cases. We must look instead to the effect of segregation itself on public education.
>
> In approaching this problem, we cannot turn the clock back to 1868 when the Amendment was adopted, or even to 1896 when *Plessy* v. *Ferguson* was written. We must consider public education in the light of its full development and its present place in American life throughout the Nation.

Only in this way can it be determined if segregation in public schools deprives these plaintiffs of the equal protection of the laws.

Today, education is perhaps the most important function of state and local governments. Compulsory school attendance laws and the great expenditures for education both demonstrate our recognition of the importance of education to our democratic society. It is required in the performance of our most basic public responsibilities, even service in the armed forces. It is the very foundation of good citizenship. Today it is a principal instrument in awakening the child to cultural values, in preparing him for later professional training, and in helping him to adjust normally to his environment. In these days, it is doubtful that any child may reasonably be expected to succeed in life if he is denied the opportunity of an education. Such an opportunity, where the state has undertaken to provide it, is a right which must be made available to all on equal terms.

We come then to the question presented: Does segregation of children in public schools solely on the basis of race, even though the physical facilities and other "tangible" factors may be equal, deprive the children of the minority group of equal educational opportunities? We believe that it does.

In *Sweatt* v. *Painter*, in finding that a segregated law school for Negroes could not provide them equal educational opportunities, this Court relied in large part on "those qualities which are incapable of objective measurement but which made for greatness in a law school." In *McLaurin* v. *Oklahoma State Regents*, the Court, in requiring that a Negro admitted to a white graduate school be treated like all other students, again resorted to intangible considerations: ". . . his ability to study, to engage in discussions and exchange views with other students, and, in general, to learn his profession." Such considerations apply with added force to children in grade and high schools. To separate them from others of similar age and qualifications solely because of their race generates a feeling of inferiority as to their status in the community that may affect their hearts and minds in a way unlikely ever to be undone. The effect of this separation on their educational opportunities was well stated by a finding in the Kansas case by a court which nevertheless felt compelled to rule against the Negro plaintiffs: "Segregation of white and colored children in public schools has a detrimental effect upon the colored children. The impact is greater when it has the sanction of law; for the policy of separating the races is usually interpreted as denoting the inferiority of the negro [*sic*] group. A sense of inferiority affects the motivation of a child to learn. Segregation with the sanction of law, therefore, has a tendency to [retard] the educational and mental development of negro [*sic*] children and to deprive them of some of the benefits they would receive in a

racially integrated school system."
Whatever may have been the extent of
psychological knowledge at the time of
Plessy v. *Ferguson*, this finding is amply
supported by modern authority. Any
language in *Plessy* v. *Ferguson* contrary to
this finding is rejected.

We conclude that in the field of public
education the doctrine of "separate but
equal" has no place. Separate educational
facilities are inherently unequal. Therefore,
we hold the plaintiffs and others similarly
situated for whom the actions have been
brought are, by reason of the segregation
complained of, deprived of the equal
protection of the laws guaranteed by the
Fourteenth Amendment. (*Id.* at 492-95)

Significance of the Decision. Despite the diversity
of opinion and attitude throughout the nation
regarding the Court's decision in *Brown*, it is
significant that the decision was *unanimous*. In
contrast to the *split* decisions pertaining to the issues
of religious influences in the public schools and the
academic freedom of teachers, there was not a single
dissent to the opinion delivered by Chief Justice
Warren.

That such unanimity would not be displayed by
the general public was expected by the Court.
Although holding firm that all provisions of federal,
state, or local law requiring or permitting
discrimination had to yield to the decision, the Court
realized that further consideration had to be given to
the manner in which relief could be afforded.

Consequently a subsequent case (*Brown* v. *Board*

of Education, 349 U.S. 294, 75 S. Ct. 753, 1955) was initiated for the purpose of implementing the *Brown I* decision of 1954. Because of the nationwide significance of the decision, the Court invited the Attorney General of the United States and the attorneys general of all states requiring or permitting racial discrimination in public education to present their views for resolving issues that lay ahead. After hearing a number of briefs, the Court arrived at a decision and remanded the cases to district courts "to take such proceedings and enter such orders and decrees consistent with their opinion as are necessary and proper to admit to public schools on a nondiscriminatory basis with all deliberate speed the parties to these cases."

Noteworthy in Warren's briefing were suggested guidelines to follow in the interests of the plaintiffs:

> ... the courts may consider problems related to administration, arising from the physical condition of the school plant, the school transportation system, personnel, revision of school districts and attendance areas into compact units to achieve a system of determining admission to the public schools on a nonracial basis, and revision of local laws and regulations which may be necessary in solving the foregoing problems. They will also consider the adequacy of any plans the defendants may propose to meet these problems and to effectuate a transition to a racially nondiscriminatory school system. During this period of

transition, the courts will retain jurisdiction of these cases. (349 U.S. at 300-1)

The above quotation from the Court indicates that many questions remained unresolved and that much litigation would follow. Consequently, scores of cases have gone to the lower federal courts. Some have been appealed to and ruled upon by the Supreme Court—several of which are to be discussed in subsequent chapters of this publication.

Chapter 12

DEFIANCE OF DESEGREGATION ORDER

(held unconstitutional)

Cooper v. *Aaron* (Ark.), 358 U.S. 1, 78 S. Ct. 1401 (1958)

The Issue. The issue, briefly stated, was whether the Legislature and Governor of the State of Arkansas, opposing desegregation of the races in the public schools, could lawfully defy the Federal Court order to desegregate in accordance with the *Brown* decision.

Background. Following the *Brown* decisions of 1954 and 1955, the Little Rock School Board adopted a policy for desegregation. The Superintendent of Schools submitted a plan whereby integration would begin at the senior high school in 1957, and then continue through the junior high schools and elementary schools, with all levels to be segregated by 1963.

"While the School Board was thus going forward with its preparation for desegregating the Little Rock school system, other state authorities, in contrast, were actively pursuing a program designed to perpetuate in Arkansas the system of racial segregation which this Court had held violated the Fourteenth Amendment." (358 U.S. at 8)

The School Board and the Superintendent of Schools nevertheless continued with preparation to carry out the first stage of the desegregation program. But the Negroes were dissatisfied with the slow pace proposed for desegregation and accordingly instituted litigation for relief.

Then in early 1958, the School Board and Superintendent of Schools filed a petition in the District Court seeking a postponement of their planned program for desegregation. Because of the "extreme public hostility" engendered largely by the official attitudes of the Governor and the Legislature, the Board proposed that the Negro students already admitted to the school be withdrawn and sent to segregated school, and that all further steps to carry out the Board's desegregation program be postponed for a period later suggested by the Board to be two and one-half years. After a hearing, the District Court found the situation so "intolerable" that it granted the relief requested by the Board.

As was to be expected, Negro respondents appealed to the Court of Appeals for the Eighth Circuit Court seeking a stay of the District Court's judgment. After considerable judicial maneuvering, the Circuit Court reversed the judgment of the District Court. On further appeal the case then went to the United States Supreme Court.

U. S. Supreme Court Decision. On September 29, 1958, the United States Supreme Court was unanimous in its decision which affirmed the Circuit Court in that a Legislature and Governor of a state were powerless to obstruct rulings of the Federal Court.

In speaking for the Court, Chief Justice Warren stated:

No state legislator or executive or judicial officer can war against the Constitution without violating his undertaking to support it. Chief Justice Marshall spoke for a unanimous Court in saying that: "If the legislatures of the several states may, at will, annul the judgments of the courts of the United States, and destroy the rights acquired under those judgments, the constitution itself becomes a solemn mockery. . . ." A governor who asserts a power to nullify a federal court order is similarly restrained. If he had such power, said Chief Justice Hughes, in 1932, also for a unanimous Court, "it is manifest that the fiat of a State Governor, and not the Constitution of the United States, would be the supreme power of the land; that the restrictions of the Federal Constitution upon the exercise of state power would be but impotent phrases. . . ."

It is, of course, quite true that the responsibility for public education is primarily the concern of the States, but it is equally true that such responsibilities, like all other state activity, must be exercised consistently with federal constitutional requirements as they apply to state action. The Constitution created a government dedicated to equal justice under law. The Fourteenth Amendment embodied and emphasized that ideal. State support of segregated schools through any arrangement, management, funds or prop-

erty cannot be squared with the Amendment's command that no State shall deny
to any person within its jurisdiction the
equal protection of the laws. The right of
a student not to be segregated on racial
grounds in schools so maintained is indeed
so fundamental and pervasive that it is
embraced in the concept of due process of
law. The basic decision in *Brown* was
unanimously reached by this Court only
after the case had been briefed and twice
argued and the issues had been given the
most serious consideration. Since the first
Brown opinion three new Justices have
come to the Court. They are at one with the
Justices still in the Court who participated
in that basic decision as to its correctness,
and that decision is now unanimously
reaffirmed. The principles announced in
that decision and the obedience of the States
to them, according to the command of the
Constitution, are indispensable for the
protection of the freedoms guaranteed by
our fundamental charter for all of us. Our
constitutional ideal of equal justice under
law is thus made a living truth. (*Id.* at 18-20)

In a concurring opinion, Justice Frankfurter
further stressed the gravity of a situation such as
was evidenced in Little Rock:

The use of force to further obedience to
law is in any event a last resort and one not
congenial to the spirit of our Nation. But the
tragic aspect of this disruptive tactic was
that the power of the State was used not to
sustain law but as an instrument for
thwarting law. The State of Arkansas is

thus responsible for disabling one of its
subordinate agencies, the Little Rock School
Board, from peacefully carrying out the
Board's and State's constitutional duty. . . .
Violent resistance to law cannot be made a
legal reason for its suspension without
loosening the fabric of our society. What
could this mean but to acknowledge that
disorder under the aegis of a State has
moral superiority over the law of the
Constitution? For those in authority thus to
defy the law of the land is profoundly
subversive not only of our constitutional
system but of the presuppositions of a
democratic society. (*Id.* at 21-2)

In conclusion, Justice Frankfurter declared:

That the responsibility of those who
exercise power in a democratic government
is not to reflect inflamed public feeling but
to help form its understanding, is especially
true when they are confronted with a
problem like a racially discriminating public
school system. This is a lesson to be drawn
from the heartening experience in ending
enforced racial segregation in the public
schools in cities with Negro populations of
large proportions. Compliance with
decisions of this Court, as the constitutional
organ of the Supreme Law of the Land, has
often, throughout our history, depended on
active support by state and local authorities.
It presupposes such support. To withhold it,
and indeed to use political power to try to
paralyze the Supreme Law, precludes the
maintenance of our federal system as we

have known and cherished it for one hundred and seventy years. (*Id.* at 26)

Significance of the Decision. Although comparatively little publicity has been given, in recent years, to *Cooper* v. *Aaron*, it must be regarded as one of the important landmark decisions. If the Supreme Court had upheld the defiant action of the Legislature and Governor of Arkansas, the very foundation of our federal government would have suffered. The decision in *Brown*, which struck down segregation of the races in the public schools, would have been nullified; the United States Constitution, which designates the United States Supreme Court as final arbiter to legal disputes, would have been ignored; and, in fact, the whole federal system of government, which has prevailed for nearly two centuries, would have been in jeopardy.

Very few, if any, United States Supreme Court cases can be found where the Court's comments are more forceful in denouncing blatant efforts of public officials to thwart constitutional justice. It is inconceivable that legislators and governors themselves would not know that state power is subordinate to that of the federal government in matters concerning civil rights. Of course, an objective to win support of the electorate which shares opposition to the "law of the land" could have been a motivating factor in this case.

The decision in *Cooper* v. *Aaron* did not terminate entirely the actions of some public officials to defy the judicial ruling in *Brown*—as has been exemplified by establishing picket lines and blocking passage to school buildings. Such efforts, however, are nullified before reaching litigation at the United States Supreme Court level. Less dramatic attempts to circumvent the *Brown* ruling, however, still continue—some of which do raise constitutional questions to be resolved by the Supreme Court, and which will be reported in subsequent chapters of this publication.

Chapter 13

DISMISSAL FOR REFUSAL TO
REVEAL ASSOCIATION

(held constitutional)

Beilan v. *Board of Education* (Pa.), 357
U.S. 399, 78 S. Ct. 1317 (1958)

The Issue. The issue in this case, as conceived by
the Court, was "whether the Board of Public
Education for the School District of Philadelphia,
Pennsylvania, violated the Due Process Clause of the
Fourteenth Amendment to the Constitution of the
United States when the Board, purporting to act
under Pennsylvania Public School Codes, discharged
a public school teacher on the ground of
'incompetency' evidenced by the teacher's refusal of
the Superintendent's request to confirm or refute
information as to the teacher's loyalty and his
activities in certain allegedly subversive organizations." (357 U.S. at 400)

Background. On June 25, 1952, Herman A. Beilan,
who had been a teacher for about twenty-two years
in the Philadelphia School System, presented himself
at his Superintendent's office in response to the
latter's request. The Superintendent said he had
information which reflected adversely to his
(Beilan's) loyalty and he wanted to determine its
truth or falsity. The Superintendent then asked
Beilan whether or not he had been an officer of the
Communist Political Association. Beilan was

granted permission to consult counsel before answering the question.

Several months later, after having consulted with his counsel, Beilan declined to answer that question or others of that type, as was his privilege in accordance with the Fifth Amendment.

Beilan's refusal to answer was construed by the Board to constitute "incompetency." Since the Pennsylvania statutes do not have a "catch-all" phrase such as "unbecoming conduct" as a reason for dismissing teachers, the Pennsylvania courts have, on several occasions, given a broad interpretation to the word "incompetency." Consequently, on January 7, 1954, the Board found that the charge of incompetency had been sustained and accordingly discharged Beilan from his employment as a teacher.

On an administrative appeal, the Superintendent of Public Instruction of Pennsylvania sustained the local Board. However, on Beilan's appeal to the County Court of Common Pleas, the court set aside Beilan's discharge and held that the Board should have followed the procedure specified by the Pennsylvania Loyalty Act, rather than the Public School Code. Finally, on the Board's appeal, "the Supreme Court of Pennsylvania, with two justices dissenting, reversed the Court of Common Pleas and reinstated petitioner's (Beilan's) discharge." (*Id.* at 404). With the granting of certiorari, the case then went to the United States Supreme Court for a final ruling.

U. S. Supreme Court Decision. In a five to four decision, with Justice Burton writing for the majority, the High Court sustained the state Supreme Court, and thereby held that *Beilan's discharge did not violate the Due Process Clause of the Fourteenth Amendment.*

Justice Burton wrote: "By engaging in teaching in the public schools, petitioner (Beilan) did not give up his right to freedom of belief, speech or association. He did, however, undertake obligations of frankness, candor and cooperation in answering inquiries made of him by his employing Board examining into his fitness to serve it as a public school teacher." (*Id.* at 405)

The Justice supported the above legal principle with the following classic passage quoted from *Adler* v. *Board of Education, supra.*

> A teacher works in a sensitive area in a schoolroom. There he shapes the attitudes of young minds towards the society in which they live. In this, the state has a vital concern. It must preserve the integrity of the schools. That the school authorities have the right and the duty to screen officials, teachers, and employees as to their fitness to maintain the integrity of the schools, as a part of ordered society, cannot be doubted. (*Id.* at 405)

Justice Burton then added:

> The Board based its dismissal upon petitioner's refusal to answer any inquiry about his relevant activities—not upon those activities themselves. It took care to charge petitioner with incompetency, and not with disloyalty. It found him

insubordinate and lacking in frankness and candor—it made no finding as to his loyalty.

We find no requirement in the Federal Constitution that a teacher's classroom conduct be the sole basis for determining his fitness. Fitness for teaching depends on a broad range of factors. (*Id.* at 406)

After noting that the teacher's employment was not terminated on the charge of disloyalty, Justice Frankfurter, in a concurring opinion, emphasized that Beilan's discharge was because "... governmental authorities, like other employers, sought to satisfy themselves of the dependability of employees in relation to their duties. Accordingly, they made inquiries that, it is not contradicted, could in and of themselves be made. These inquiries were balked. The services of the employees were therefore terminated." (*Id.* at 410)

Chief Justice Warren and Justices Douglas, Black, and Brennan dissented. Justice Brennan, whose dissent was the lengthiest stressed that in the case at hand: "It is obvious that more is at stake here than the loss of position of public employment for unreliability or incompetence. Rather it is the simultaneous public labeling of the employees as disloyal that gives rise to our concern." (*Id.* at 418)

Significance of the Decision. Several other school cases, dealing with the right of association, have come before the United States Supreme Court for settlement. Most of them, however, deal with the issue of the requirement of signing oaths of non-affiliation. The *Beilan* case is the only one reaching the Supreme Court where a teacher, at the high-school level, has employed the strategem of invoking the Fifth Amendment to conceal affiliation with subversive organizations.

Although the Supreme Court ruled, in 1952, (*Adler, supra*) that a teacher could be dismissed for refusing to sign an oath of non-affiliation with allegedly subversive organizations, other cases still to be reported, indicate teachers cannot now be discharged merely for refusing to reveal their affiliation with such organizations.

The *Beilan* case was litigated between the period when the Court ruled that teachers were compelled to reveal their association and the period when they were not compelled to do so. Consequently there was diversity of opinion, both by the public and the judiciary, regarding the issue. The indefiniteness of the judiciary is indicated by the split five to four decision. However, had the *Beilan* case been decided on the basis of loyalty rather than insubordination, the decision might have been different.

The decision was criticized by many. The dissenting justices, as wel¹ as others who have written about the case, argue that Beilan was denied his constitutional rights. As support for their claim they cite numerous former cases in which the teacher was judicially allowed to invoke the Fifth Amendment when questioned about subversive connections. It should be noted, however, that the other cases concerned teachers at the college level, whereas the *Beilan* case involved a high school teacher. That age level could be an influential factor is supported by a statement from a state court: "a teacher's conduct outside of the classroom is less important . . . in high school than in the grammar school. . . ." (*Kaplan* v. *School District of Philadelphia*, 388 Pa. 213, 130 A.2d 672, at 680, 1957). So, had Beilan been teaching at the grammar or elementary level, the case against him would have been still stronger.

Chapter 14

REQUIREMENT FOR RECITATION
OF STATE PRAYER

(held unconstitutional)

Engel v. *Vitale* (N.Y.), 370 U.S. 421, 82
S. Ct. 1261 (1962)

The Issue. The issue here is whether state officials
may constitutionally compose an official state prayer
and require that it be recited in the public schools of
the State at the beginning of each school day—even if
the prayer is denominationally neutral and if pupils
who wish to do so may remain silent or be excused
from the room while the prayer is being recited.

Background. This case was brought into focus
when the State Board of Regents composed a brief
prayer which they recommended for the public
schools of New York: "Almighty God, we
acknowledge our dependence upon Thee, and we beg
Thy blessing upon us, our parents, our teachers and
our Country."

Shortly after the practice of reciting the Regents'
prayer was adopted by the school district of New
Hyde Park, the parents of ten pupils brought action
in a state court—insisting that the official prayer in
the public schools was contrary to the beliefs,
religions, or religious practices of both themselves
and their children. They further contended that the
district's regulation ordering the recitation of this
particular prayer was a violation of the First

Amendment of the Federal Constitution, which was "made applicable to the State of New York by the Fourteenth Amendment of said Constitution."

Despite the above charges, the recitation of the Regents' prayer as required by the school district was held legal by the Court of Appeals of New York State. However, it was appealed to the United States Supreme Court for final judgment.

U. S. Supreme Court Decision. On June 25, 1962, the United States Supreme Court rendered its decision that *the requirement of the recital of a state-composed prayer in the public school classroom was in violation of the Establishment Clause of the First Amendment.* The opinion of the Court was written by Justice Black. Justices Frankfurter and White did not participate in the opinion. Justice Stewart was the lone dissenter.

In speaking for the majority, Justice Black stated:

> We think that by using its public school system to encourage recitation of the Regents' prayer, the State of New York has adopted a practice wholly inconsistent with the Establishment Clause. There can, of course, be no doubt that New York's program of daily classroom invocation of God's blessings as prescribed in the Regents' prayer is a religious activity. It is a solemn avowal of divine faith and supplication for the blessings of the Almighty. The nature of such a prayer has always been religious. . . . (370 U.S. at 424)
>
> The petitioners contend among other things that the state laws requiring or permitting use of the Regents' prayer must

be struck down as a violation of the Establishment Clause because that prayer was composed by governmental officials as a part of a governmental program to further religious beliefs. For this reason, petitioners argue, the State's use of the Regents' prayer in its public school system breaches the constitutional wall of separation between Church and State. We agree with that contention since we think that the constitutional prohibition against laws respecting an establishment of religion must at least mean that in this country it is no part of the business of government to compose official prayers for any group of the American people to recite as a part of a religious program carried on by government.

It is a matter of history that this very practice of establishing governmentally composed prayers for religious services was one of the reasons which caused many of our early colonists to leave England and seek religious freedom in America. ... (*Id.* at 425)

After reciting the historical background of religious controversy in England, which prompted the colonists to seek religious freedom in America, Justice Black continued thusly:

There can be no doubt that New York's state prayer program officially establishes the religious beliefs embodied in the Regents' prayer. The respondents' argument to the contrary, which is largely based upon the contention that the Regents' prayer is "non-denominational" and the fact that the program, as modified and approved by state courts, does not require all pupils to recite the prayer but permits those who wish to do so to remain silent or be excused from the room, ignore the essential nature of the program's constitutional defects. Neither the fact that the prayers may be denominationally neutral nor the fact that its observance on the part of students is voluntary can serve to free it from the limitations of the Establishment Clause, as it might from the Free Exercise Clause, of the First Amendment, both of which are operative against the States by virtue of the Fourteenth Amendment. Although these two clauses may in certain instances overlap, they forbid two quite different kinds of governmental encroachment upon religious freedom. The Establishment Clause, unlike the Free Exercise, does not depend upon any showing of direct governmental compulsion and is violated by the enactment of laws which establish an official religion whether those laws operate directly to coerce non-observing individuals or not. This is not to say, of course, that laws officially prescribing a particular form of religious worship do not involve coercion of such individuals. When the power, prestige and financial support of government is placed behind a particular religious belief, the indirect coercive pressure upon religious minorities to conform to the prevailing officially approved religion is plain. But the purposes underlying the Establishment Clause go much further than that. Its first and most immediate purpose rested on the belief that a union of government and religion tends to destroy government and to degrade religion. The history of governmentally established religion, both in England and in this country, showed that whenever government has allied itself with one particular form of religion, the inevitable result had been that it had incurred the hatred, disrespect and even contempt of those who held contrary beliefs. That same history showed that many people had lost their respect for any religion that had relied upon the support of government to spread its faith. ... (*Id.* at 430-31)

In refuting the view that because the Regents' official prayer is so brief and general there can be no danger to religious freedom in its governmental establishment, Justice Black concludes his remarks by quoting the following passage from James Madison, the author of the First Amendment:

It is proper to take alarm at the first experiment on our liberties. ... Who does not see that the same authority which can establish Christianity, in exclusion of all other Religions, may establish with the same ease any particular sect of Christians, in exclusion of all other Sects? That the same authority which can force a citizen to contribute three pence only of his property for the support of any one establishment, may force him to conform to any other's establishment in all cases whatsoever. (*Id.* at 436)

In a concurring opinion, Justice Douglas stressed the financial aspects of the case in these words:

> In New York the teacher who leads in prayer is on the public payroll; and the time she takes seems minuscule as compared with the salaries appropriated by state legislatures and Congress for chaplains to conduct prayers in the legislative halls. Only a bare fraction of the teacher's time is given to reciting this short twenty-two-word prayer, about the same amount of time that our Crier spends announcing the opening of our sessions and offering a prayer for this Court. Yet for me the principle is the same, no matter how briefly the prayer is said, for in each of the instances given the person praying is a public official on the public payroll, performing a religious exercise in a governmental institution. . . . (*Id.* at 441)

Justice Stewart, although not joined by others, filed a vigorous dissent as indicated by the following passages:

> The Court does not hold, nor could it, that New York has interfered with the free exercise of anybody's religion. For the state courts have made clear that those who object to reciting the prayer must be entirely free of any compulsion to do so, including any "embarrassments and pressures." But the Court says that in permitting school children to say this simple prayer, the New York authorities have established "an official religion."
>
> With all respect, I think the Court has misapplied a great constitutional principle.

I cannot see how an "official religion" is established by letting those who want to say a prayer say it. On the contrary, I think that to deny the wish of these school children to join in reciting this prayer is to deny them the opportunity of sharing in the spiritual heritage of our Nation. (*Id.* at 445)

I do not believe that this Court, or the Congress, or the President has by the actions and practices I have mentioned established an "official religion" in violation of the Constitution. And I do not believe the State of New York has done so in this case. What each has done has been to recognize and to follow the deeply entrenched and highly cherished spiritual traditions of our Nation—traditions which come down to us from those who almost two hundred years ago avowed their "firm Reliance on the Protection of divine Providence," when they proclaimed the freedom and independence of this brave new world.

I dissent. (*Id.* at 450)

Significance of the Decision. The decision in this case had to do with an *official state prayer*—leaving doubt as to legality of reciting school prayers that are not officially designed. Since the Supreme Court did not specifically invalidate the recitation of all prayers in all situations, some school officials and teachers have attempted to continue the practice in a minor degree.

Consequently litigation on the issue continues. A case originating in Illinois is illustrative (*De Spain* v. *De Kalb County Community School District,* 384 F.2d 836, 1968). Here a United States Court of

Appeals reversed a federal district court's ruling which upheld the recitation of a brief verse (prayer) by children in a kindergarten class before their morning snack. In commenting on the case, the Court of Appeals stated: "We are of the view that the verse is a prayer and that its compulsory recitation by kindergarten students in a public school comes within the proscription of the first amendment, as interpreted by the Supreme Court in the "school prayer" cases. (*Id.* at 837)

The Court recognized the "commendable virtues" in teaching "good manners" and "gratitude" but concluded that "any religious activity of whatever nature could be justified by public officials on the basis that the activity has beneficial secular purposes; as a result the Supreme Court's admonition in *Engel* and *Schempp* would be meaningless." (*Id.* at 839)

According to the ruling in *De Spain*, then, it would appear that the ruling in *Engel* is broad enough to void *mandated* prayers, regardless of whether they are mandated by *state officials* or by classroom teachers. However, nothing in the court rulings thus far prohibits *voluntary prayers.*

Since the *Engel* decision was almost unanimous (only Justice Stewart dissenting) it is not likely that the Court will veer from its 1962 ruling. Those who read the entire opinion of the Court will understand why. About the only way in which a Supreme Court ruling would uphold the recitation of mandated prayers in the public schools would be by amendment to the Constitution. That appears unlikely and unwise, despite the fact that many holding high political office are suggesting it. It is unfortunate that the issue has developed into a "political football."

Chapter 15

REQUIREMENT TO READ PASSAGES FROM THE BIBLE IN THE PUBLIC SCHOOLS

(held unconstitutional)

Abington School District v. *Schempp* (Pa.), 374 U.S. 203, 83 S. Ct. 1560 (1963)

The Issue. The issue in this case is whether a state law or school board may constitutionally require that passages of the Bible be read or that the Lord's Prayer be recited in the public schools—even if individual students may be excused from attending or participating in such exercises upon written request of their parents.

Background. The issue of Bible reading in the public schools had been litigated in the lower courts for nearly a century, and, until 1963, there had been a preponderance of jurisdiction validating the practice—particularly where pupil participation was optional.

Controversy and litigation over the issue reached a climax in 1963 when the constitutionality of a Pennsylvania statute was challenged which required that: "at least ten verses from the Holy Bible be read, without comment, at the opening of each public school on each day." During the process of litigation, the original statutory regulation was amended by adding the exemption clause that: "Any child shall be excused from such Bible reading upon the written request of his parent or guardian."

The Schempp family (Unitarians), husband and wife and two of their three children, brought suit to enjoin enforcement of the statute, contending that "their rights under the Fourteenth Amendment to the Constitution of the United States are, have been, and will continue to be violated unless this statute be declared unconstitutional as violative of these provisions of the First Amendment." (274 U.S. at 205)

This was the first case, regarding the Bible-reading issue, that reached the federal courts. In upholding the Schempps' contentions, a three-judge District Court ruled that the statute was violative of the Establishment Clause of the First Amendment. On appeal the case then went to the United States Supreme Court.

U. S. Supreme Court Decision. The Supreme Court took the *Schempp* case along with its companion (*Murray* v. *Curlett, Constituting the Board of School Commissioners of Baltimore City,* 179 A.2d 698, 1962) involving almost identical issues. Therefore, the decision reached by the United States Supreme Court applied to both cases.

On June 17, 1963, the High Court affirmed the lower court ruling and stated that: "In light of the history of the First Amendment and of our cases interpreting and applying its requirements, we hold that the practices at issue and the laws requiring them are unconstitutional under the Establishment Clause, as applied to the States through the Fourteenth Amendment." (274 U.S. at 205)

Justice Clark, who delivered the opinion of the

Court, placed stress and confirmation upon the following comment of the trial court:

> The reading of the verses, even without comment, possesses a devotional and religious character and constitutes in effect a religious observance. The devotional and religious nature of the morning exercise is made all the more apparent by the fact that the Bible reading is followed immediately by a recital in unison by the pupils of the Lord's Prayer. The fact that some pupils, or theoretically all pupils, might be excused from attendance at the exercises does not mitigate the obligatory nature of the ceremony. . . . The exercises are held in the school buildings and perforce are conducted by and under the authority of the local school authorities and during school sessions. Since the statute requires the reading of the "Holy Bible" a Christian document, the practice . . . prefers the Christian religion. (*Id* at 210-11)

In commenting on the alleged secular purpose of the religious exercises in the public schools, Justice Clark stated:

> But even if its purpose is not strictly religious, it is sought to be accomplished through readings, without comment, from the Bible. Surely the place of the Bible as an instrument of religion cannot be gainsaid, and the State's recognition of the pervading religious character of the ceremony is evident from the rule's specific permission of the alternative use of the Catholic Douay version as well as the recent amendment

permitting nonattendance at the exercises. None of these factors is consistent with the contention that the Bible is here used either as an instrument for nonreligious moral inspiration or as a reference for the teaching of secular subjects. (*Id.* at 224)

The concluding remark of Justice Clark indicates the high regard the Court holds for religion in our society:

The place of religion in our society is an exalted one, achieved through a long tradition of reliance on the home, the church and the inviolable citadel of the individual heart and mind. We have come to recognize through bitter experience that it is not within the power of government to invade that citadel, whether its purpose or effect be to aid or oppose, to advance or retard. In the relationship between man and religion, the State is firmly committed to a position of neutrality. Though the application of that rule requires interpretation of a delicate sort, the rule is clearly and concisely stated in the words of the First Amendment. (*Id.* at 226)

Justice Douglas, who has considered the financial ramifications of all cases concerning church-school relations, states in his concurring opinion the following:

... the Establishment Clause is not limited to precluding the State itself from conducting religious exercises. It also forbids the State to employ its facilities or funds in a way that gives any church, or all churches, greater strength in our society than it would have by relying on its members alone. Thus, the present regimes must fall under that clause for the additional reason that public funds, though small in amount, are being used to promote a religious exercise. Through the mechanism of the State, all of the people are being required to finance a religious exercise that only some of the people want and that violates the sensibilities of others. (*Id.* at 229)

Such contributions may not be made by the State even in a minor degree without violating the Establishment Clause. It is not the amount of public funds expanded; as this case illustrates, it is the use to which public funds are put that is controlling. For the First Amendment does not say that some forms of establishment are allowed; it says that "no law respecting an establishment of religion" shall be made. What may be done directly may not be done indirectly lest the Establishment Clause becomes a mockery. (*Id.* at 230)

Justice Brennan in a very lengthy concurring opinion (75 pages) traced the history of preceding religious cases as related to the First Amendment. Then with respect to the *Schempp* and *Murray* cases before the Court, he stated:

The religious nature of the exercises here challenged seems plain. Unless *Engel* v. *Vitale* is to be overruled, or we are to engage in wholly disingenuous distinction, we cannot sustain these practices. Daily recital

of the Lord's Prayer and the reading of
passages of Scripture are quite as clearly
breaches of the command of the
Establishment Clause as was the daily use
of the rather bland Regents' Prayer in the
New York public schools. Indeed, I would
suppose that, if anything, the Lord's Prayer
and the Holy Bible are more clearly
sectarian, and the present violations of the
First Amendment consequently more
serious. (*Id.* at 266-7)

Justice Goldberg, joined by Justice Harlan, in still
another concurring opinion agreed that the attitude
of government toward religion must be one of
neutrality. He stated:

Neither government nor this Court can or
should ignore the significance of the fact
that a vast portion of our people believe in
and worship God and that many of our
legal, political and personal values derive
historically from religious teachings.
Government must inevitably take
cognizance of the existence of religion and,
indeed, under certain circumstances the
First Amendment may require that it do so.
And it seems clear to me from the opinions
in the present and past cases that the Court
would recognize the propriety of providing
military chaplains and of the teaching *about*
religion, as distinguished from the teaching
of religion, in the public schools. The
examples could readily be multiplied, for
both the required and the permissible
accommodations between state and church
frame the relation as one free of hostility or
favor and productive of religious and

political harmony, but without undue involvement of one in the concerns or practices of the other. To be sure, the judgment in each case is a delicate one, but it must be made if we are to do loyal service as judges to the ultimate First Amendment objective of religious liberty. (*Id.* at 306)

As in the preceding case (*Engel* v. *Vitale*), Justice Stewart was the lone dissenter. In refuting arguments of the majority, he emphasized that:

It might also be argued that parents who want their children exposed to religious influences can adequately fulfil that wish off school property and outside school time. With all its surface persuasiveness, however, this argument seriously misconceives the basic constitutional justification for permitting the exercises at issue in these cases. For a compulsory state educational system so structures a child's life that if religious exercises are held to be an impermissible activity in schools, religion is placed at an artificial and state-created disadvantage. Viewed in this light, permission of such exercises for those who want them is necessary if the schools are truly to be neutral in the matter of religion. And a refusal to permit religious exercises thus is seen, not as the realization of state neutrality, but rather as the establishment of a religion of secularism, or at the least, as government support of the beliefs of those who think that religious exercises should be conducted only in private. (*Id.* at 313)

Significance of the Decision. Like in other cases

involving religious activities in public schools, the Supreme Court has been consistent in voiding the activities. Therefore, it may be concluded from the church-school decisions thus far that any religious activity in the public schools which collides with the Establishment Clause of the First Amendment will be declared unconstitutional. And as brought out in the arguments, the fact that the statute requires the reading of the "Holy Bible, a Christian document, a preference for religious beliefs is established."

It is difficult to conceive a religious ceremony program conducted in the public schools that would meet with general approval by the multitude of religious and antireligious attitudes and faiths represented in the public. It would be extremely difficult to avoid favoritism.

It should be pointed out that the Court has not taken an "antireligious" stance in its decisions but, rather, a "nonreligious" position—which is one of neutrality as required by the Constitution.

Significantly the Court did not outlaw the Bible as a document for secular educational purposes. Justice Goldberg, in his concurring opinion, differentiated between the *legal* practice of teaching *about religion* as contrasted with the *illegal* teaching *of religion.*

Since the Court implied, in the *Schempp* decision, that the study of the Bible may be presented objectively in a secular program of education, school authorities have been in a quandry as to how far they may go in teaching *about* religion without violating the First Amendment. A federal court, in ruling on a Martinsville, Virginia, case (*Vaughn* v. *Reed*, 313 F.

Supp. 431, 1970), summarized an acceptable plan for a school district as follows:

> The court sustains the position of plaintiff that no religious education program should be conducted in the public schools which employs material or practices which would amount to an indoctrination of religion. At the same time the court holds that a program encompassing all students controlled by the school authorities and practices without indoctrination of religion is not unconstitutional, all of which is adjudged and ordered. (*Id.* at 434)

Chapter 16

OATH REQUIREMENT OF NON-AFFILIATION WITH SUBVER-SIVE ORGANIZATIONS

(held unconstitutional)

Elfbrandt v. *Russell* (Ariz.), 384 U.S.
11, 87 S. Ct. 1238 (1966)

The Issue. The issue in this case concerns the constitutionality of an Arizona Act requiring an oath from state employees (including public-school teachers) that they are not knowingly members of the Communist Party or a subversive organization.

Background. The oath involved in the litigation was of conventional pattern as to the support of the United States Constitution and the Constitution of Arizona. The oath reads as follows:

> I do solemnly swear that I will support the Constitution of the United States and the Constitution and laws of the State of Arizona; that I will bear true faith and allegiance to the same, and defend them against all enemies, foreign and domestic, and that I will faithfully and impartially discharge the duties of the office (name of office) according to the best of my ability, so help me God (or so I do affirm).

The Legislature "put a gloss on the oath" by subjecting to perjury prosecution and loss of job any state employee who took the loyalty oath and "knowingly and wilfully becomes or remains a member of the Communist party" or other organization dedicated to overthrowing the state government.

The petitioner, a teacher and a Quaker, decided she could not, in good conscience, take the oath, not knowing what it meant and being unable to obtain a hearing to determine its precise scope and meaning. She and her husband, teachers in separate schools in Tucson, refused to sign but continued to teach without being paid for nearly five years. Then litigation began.

After the Arizona Supreme Court sustained the oath, the judgment of the lower court was remanded for reconsideration in the light of *Baggett* v. *Bullitt,* 377 U.S. 360, a case which originated in the state of Washington and pertained to personnel of higher institutions. Since the lower court did not see that *Baggett* v. *Bullitt* did not apply specifically to *Elfbrandt* v. *Russell,* it stood by its original ruling. Thus by certiorari, the case went to the United States Supreme Court.

U. S. Supreme Court Decision. The United States Supreme Court, in a five to four decision, overturned the Arizona oath law. Justice Douglas, who was joined by Justices Warren, Black, Brennan and Fortas, delivered the opinion for the majority. Excerpts from the majority opinion follow:

> The oath and accompanying statutory gloss challenged here suffer from an identical constitutional infirmity. One who subscribes to this Arizona oath and who is, or thereafter becomes a knowing member of

an organization which has as "one of its purposes" the violent overthrow of the government, is subject to immediate discharge and criminal penalties. Nothing in the oath, the statutory gloss, or the construction of the oath and statutes given by the Arizona Supreme Court, purports to exclude association by one who does not subscribe to the organization's unlawful ends. (384 U.S. at 16)

Would it be legal to join a seminar group predominantly Communist, and therefore subject to control by those who are said to believe in the overthrow of the Government by force and violence? Juries might convict though the teacher did not subscribe to the wrongful aims of the organization. And there is apparently no machinery provided for getting clearance in advance.

Those who join an organization but do not share its unlawful purposes and who do not participate in its unlawful activities surely pose no threat, either as citizens or as public employees. Laws such as this which are not restricted in scope to those who join with the "specific intent" to further illegal action impose, in effect, a conclusive presumption that the member shares the unlawful aims of the organization. (*Id.* at 17)

This Act threatens the cherished freedom of association by the First Amendment, made applicable to the States through the Fourteenth Amendment.... And, as a committee of the Arizona Legislature which urged adoption of this law itself recognized, public employees of character and integrity may well forego their calling rather than risk prosecution for perjury or compromise their commitment to intellectual and political freedom:

> "The communist trained in fraud and perjury has no qualms in taking any oath; the loyal citizen, conscious of history's oppressions, may well wonder whether the medieval rack and torture wheel are next for one who declines to take an involved negative oath as evidence that he is a True Believer." (*Id.* at 18)

> A law which applies to membership without the "specific intent" to further the illegal aims of the organization infringes unnecessarily on protected freedoms. It rests on the doctrine of "guilt by association" which has no place here. Such a law cannot stand. (*Id.* at 19)

Justice White, with whom Justices Clark, Harlan and Stewart concurred, wrote a dissenting opinion which concluded with the following comment:

> Even if Arizona may not take criminal action against its law enforcement officers or its teachers who become Communists knowing of the purposes of the Party, the Court's judgment overreaches itself in invalidating this Arizona statute. Whether or not Arizona may make knowing membership a crime, it need not retain the member as an employee and is entitled to insist that its employees disclaim, under oath, knowing membership in the designated organizations and to condition future employment upon future abstention from membership. It is, therefore, improper to invalidate the entire statute in

this declaratory judgment action. If the imposition of criminal penalties under the present Act is invalid, the Court should so limit its holding and remand the case to the Arizona courts to determine the severability of the criminal provisions under the severability provisions of the Act itself. (*Id.* at 23)

Significance of the Decision. The decision in this case is significant in several respects: (1) the Court would not uphold a statute that was vague; (2) the Court differentiated between association and activity in an organization; and (3) the Court was not unanimous in its decision.

The Court refused to penalize the teachers for not signing an oath which was not clear in its meaning. *Vagueness* of an oath requirement, statutory provision, or a constitutional provision, has frequently proved to be a valid defense—particularly on the issue of academic freedom.

The First Amendment provides for the freedom of association. This freedom pertains to teachers as well as all other citizens. Guilt by association is not judicially recognized. One's activity as a member of an alleged subversive organization is the determinant of guilt.

The lack of judicial unanimity in the decision of this case is evidence that the issue of oath requirements concerning teachers' affiliation in alleged subversive organization is not settled permanently. Since this was a five to four decision, a switch of just one vote from a majority to the dissent, would have validated the oath requirement as provided for in the Arizona statute.

Chapter 17

DISMISSAL OF TEACHER FOR REFUSAL TO SIGN AFFIDAVIT OF NON-AFFILIATION WITH COMMUNIST PARTY

(held unconstitutional)

Keyishian v. *Board of Regents* (N.Y.), 385 U.S. 589, 87 S. Ct. 675 (1967)

The Issue. The issue in this case, which is quite similar to that in *Elfbrandt* v. *Russell, supra,* was whether state employees (including teachers) in New York could constitutionally be dismissed from employment for refusing to sign an affidavit stating they were not Communists. In essence, the constitutionality of the much-litigated Feinberg Law was being tested.

Background. For approximately two decades the Feinberg Law of 1949 was forceful. The Law was an implementation of an earlier Civil Service Law of New York which declared ineligible for employment in any public school any member of an organization advocating the overthrow of government by force, violence or any unlawful means.

Specifically the Feinberg Law provided that the Board of Regents, which has charge of the public school system of the state, shall, after full notice and hearing, make a listing of organizations which it finds advocate, advise, teach or embrace the doctrine that the government should be overthrown by force, violence, or any other unlawful means. The statute further authorized the Board of Regents to provide, by rule, that membership in any listed organization, after notice and hearing, "shall constitute prima facie evidence for disqualification for appointment to or retention in any office or position in the school system." (*New York Education Law*, Title V, Article 61, Sec. 3023)

Although the Feinberg Law had been litigated at the lower-court level several times, its first test in the federal courts came in 1952 when it went before the United States Supreme Court in the case of *Adler, supra.* As previously mentioned, the High Court in that case upheld the Feinberg Law and the dismissal of several teachers from their positions by the New York City Board of Education for their refusal to comply with the oath requirement stipulated in the Feinberg Law.

Here, in *Keyishian*, teachers were again dismissed for failure to sign affidavits stating they were not Communists. Following dismissal, the teachers brought action for declaratory and injunctive relief, and a three-judge federal court held the program under which they were dismissed to be constitutional. The case was then appealed to the United States Supreme Court for a final ruling.

U. S. Supreme Court Decision. The Supreme Court reversed the decision of the lower court, thereby invalidating the Feinberg Law as it applied to public school teachers. In its opinion, delivered by Justice Brennan who was joined by Justices Warren, Black, Douglas and Fortas, the Court held that the

New York statutory provision barring from
employment in public schools any person wilfully
advocating or teaching the doctrine of forcible
overthrow of the government "are unconstitutionally
vague and violate the First Amendment." By way of
emphasizing the contention that the plan was vague,
the Court stated:

> We do not have the benefit of a judicial
> gloss by the New York courts enlightening
> us as to the scope of this complicated plan.
> In light of the intricate administrative
> machinery for its enforcement, this is not
> surprising. The very intricacy of the plan
> and the uncertainty as to the scope of its
> proscriptions make it a highly efficient *in
> terrorem* mechanism. It would be a bold
> teacher who would not as far as possible
> from utterances or acts which might
> jeopardize his living by enmeshing him in
> this intricate machinery. (385 U.S. at 601)

A couple more pertinent excerpts from the Court's
opinion follow:

> There can be no doubt of the legitimacy of
> New York's interest in protecting its
> educational system from subversion. But
> "even though the governmental purpose be
> legitimate and substantial, that purpose
> cannot be pursued by means that broadly
> stifle fundamental personal liberties when
> the end can be more narrowly achieved."
> The principle is not inapplicable because the
> legislation is aimed at keeping subversives
> out of the teaching ranks. (*Id.* at 602)
> Our Nation is deeply committed to

safeguarding academic freedom, which is of transcendent value to all of us and not merely to the teachers concerned. That freedom is therefore a special concern of the First Amendment, which does not tolerate laws that cast a pall of orthodoxy over the classroom. "The vigilant protection of constitutional freedoms is nowhere more vital than in the community of American schools." The classroom is peculiarly the "marketplace of ideas." The Nation's future depends upon leaders trained through wide exposure to that robust exchange of ideas which discovers truth "out of a multitude of tongues [rather] than through any kind of authoritative selection." (*Id.* at 603)

It is noteworthy that the same Justices (Clark, Harlan, Stewart and White) who dissented in the preceding *Elfbrandt* opinion also dissented in this case.

Justice Clark wrote the dissenting opinion—the thrust of which is expressed in the following comments:

It is clear that the Feinberg Law, in which this Court found "no constitutional infirmity" in 1952, has been given its death blow today. Just as the majority here finds that there "can be no doubt of the legitimacy of New York's interest in protecting its education system from subversion" there can also be no doubt that "the be-all and end-all of New York's effort is here. And, regardless of its correctness, neither New York nor the several States that have followed the teaching of *Adler* ... for some 15 years, can ever put the pieces together again. No court has ever reached out so far to destroy so much with so little. (*Id.* at 622)

The majority says the Feinberg Law is bad because it has an "overbroad sweep." I regret to say—and I do so with deference—that the majority has by its broadside swept away one of our most precious rights, namely, the right of self-preservation. Our public educational system is the genius of our democracy. The minds of our youth are developed there and the character of that development will determine the future of our land. Indeed, our very existence depends upon it. The issue here is a very narrow one. It is not freedom of speech, freedom of thought, freedom of press, freedom of assembly or of association, even in the Communist Party. It is simply this: May the State provide that one who, after a hearing with full judicial review, is found to have wilfully and deliberately, advocated, advised, or taught that our Government should be overthrown by force or violence or other unlawful means; or to have wilfully and deliberately printed, published, etc., any book or paper that so advocated *and to have personally* advocated such doctrine himself; or to have wilfully and deliberately become a member of an organization that advocates such doctrine is prima facie disqualified from teaching in its university? My answer, in keeping with all of our cases up until today is "Yes" ! (*Id.* at 628-29)

Significance of the Decision. Considering the

closely-divided opinion on three cases pertaining to academic freedom, by refusal to sign oaths of non-affiliation with subversive organizations, it is difficult to derive a precise legal principle on the issue. The Court, in 1952, was divided six to three in upholding a statutory requirement to reveal identification with alleged subversive organizations. Next, in 1966, an Arizona Act requiring the signing of an oath was invalidated by the United States Supreme Court in a five to four decision. Then, in 1967, the Court struck down the oath requirement by another five to four decision in *Keyishian*, presently reported.

Despite the closely-divided opinions, there is a big difference in the outcome between the *Adler* decision in 1952 and the *Keyishian* decision in 1967. In the first case, the validity of the Feinberg Law which required teachers to submit an oath of non-affiliation with subversive organizations was upheld by the Court. In the latter case, however, the Court declared the Feinberg Law to be unconstitutional.

The opposite opinions, although quite evenly divided, denote a trend toward judicial rejection of vague statutory requirements for oaths of non-affiliation with subversive organizations. Some would argue that the danger of subversive infiltration in the public schools was more apparent in 1952 than it was fifteen years later; many, however, would disagree.

The big question for the Justices to decide in those cases is which is the more important and more in conformity with our Constitution: (a) the *right of self-preservation* or (b) the *freedom of association.* Although the most recent decision leans toward the freedom of association, the judicial balance could be shifted with a slight change in the constituency of the Court—the members of which are, at present, adamant in their views on the issue.

Chapter 18

DISMISSAL OF TEACHER FOR EXPRESSION OF PUBLIC CONCERN

(held unconstitutional)

Pickering v. *Board of Education* (Ill.),
391 U.S. 563, 88 S. Ct. 1731 (1968)

The Issue. In general, the issue in this case was whether public-school teachers have the constitutional right to express themselves on matters which are of public concern. More specifically, the issue was whether a teacher could be lawfully dismissed for making damaging statements about the school board's action concerning a bond issue.

Background. The case originated in Will County, Illinois, where Marvin Pickering, a teacher in a local school system, submitted a letter to the editor of a local newspaper which was critical of the way in which the board of education and the superintendent of schools had handled proposals to raise and use new revenue. Excerpts extracted from Pickering's letter to the editor depict the nature of its critical contents:

> . . . the superintendent told the teachers, and I quote, "any teacher that opposes the referendum should be prepared for the consequences." I think this gets at the reason we have problems passing bond issues. Threats take something away; these are insults to voters in a free society. We should try to sell a program on its merits, if it has any. (391 U.S. at 576)

. . . to sod football fields on borrowed money and then not be able to pay teachers' salaries is getting the cart before the horse.

If these things aren't enough for you, look at East High. No doors on many of the classrooms, a plant room without any sunlight, no water in a first aid treatment room, are just a few of many things. The taxpayers were really taken to the cleaners. A part of the sidewalk in the building has already collapsed. Maybe Mr. Hess would be interested to know that we need blinds in that building also. (*Id.* at 577)

As I see it, the bond issue is a fight between the Board of Education that is trying to push tax-supported athletics down our throats with education, and a public that has mixed emotions about both of these items because they feel they are already paying enough taxes, and simply don't know whom to trust with any more tax money.

I must sign this letter as a citizen, taxpayer and voter, not as a teacher, since that freedom has been taken from the teachers by the administration. Do you really know what goes on behind those stone walls at the high school?

Respectfully,
Marvin L. Pickering
(*Id.* at 578)

As a consequence of the above comments which were published in the local newspaper the board dismissed the teacher, claiming the letter which contained "false statements" would damage the reputation of board members and the school administration. Moreover, it was claimed the written criticism would be disruptive of faculty discipline and tend to foment controversy and conflict among the teachers, the administrators, the board of education, and the residents of the school district.

Claiming his writing of the letter was protected by the First and Fourteenth Amendments, Pickering sought review of the Board's action in the Circuit Court of Will County, which affirmed his dismissal on the ground that "the determination that appellant's letter was detrimental to the interests of the school system was supported by substantial evidence and that the interests of the schools overrode the appellant's First Amendment rights." (*Id.* at 565)

On appeal, the Supreme Court of Illinois, two Justices dissenting, affirmed the judgment of the Circuit Court. The case was then appealed to the United States Supreme Court for final settlement.

U. S. Supreme Court Decision. The High Court reversed the judgment of the Supreme Court of Illinois and ruled that Pickering could not be constitutionally dismissed from his teaching position.

In rendering its decision, the United States Supreme Court had weighed the allegations of the board, but rejected them as being inconsequential in the case where a teacher's right of free speech is involved. The rationale of the Court for its ruling is expressed in considerable length. The following excerpts from the opinion of the Court, delivered by Justice Marshall, give special emphasis to the right of school teachers to participate in public matters by exercising their right of free speech as guaranteed by the First Amendment:

> . . . the question whether a school system requires additional funds is a matter of legitimate public concern on which the judgment of the school administration, including the School Board, cannot, in a society that leaves such questions to popular vote, be taken as conclusive. On such a question free and open debate is vital to informed decision-making by the electorate. Teachers are, as a class, the members of a community most likely to have informal and definite opinions as to how funds allotted to the operation of the school should be spent. Accordingly, it is essential that they be able to speak out freely on such questions without fear of retaliatory dismissal. (*Id.* at 571-72)

> What we do have before us is a case in which a teacher has made erroneous public statements upon issues then currently the subject of public attention, which are critical of his ultimate employer but which are neither shown nor can be presumed to have in any way either impeded the teacher's proper performance of his daily duties in the classroom or to have interfered with the regular operation of the schools generally. In these circumstances we conclude that the interest of the school administration in limiting teachers' opportunities to contribute to public debate is not significantly greater than its interest in limiting a similar contribution by any member of the general public. (*Id.* at 572-73)

While criminal sanction and damage awards have a somewhat different impact on the exercise of the right to freedom of speech from dismissal from employment, it is apparent that the threat of dismissal from public employment is nonetheless a potent means of inhibiting speech. We have already noted our disinclination to make an across-the-board equation of dismissal from public employment for remarks critical of superiors with awarding damages in a libel suit by a public official for similar criticism. However, in a case such as the present one, in which the fact of employment is only tangentially and insubstantially involved in the subject matter of the public communication made by a teacher, we conclude that it is necessary to regard the teacher as the member of the general public he seeks to be.

In sum, we hold that, in a case such as this, absent proof of false statements knowingly or recklessly made by him, a teacher's exercise of his right to speak on issues of public importance may not furnish the basis for his dismissal from public employment. Since no such showing has been made in this case regarding appellant's letter, his dismissal for writing it cannot be upheld and the judgment of the Illinois Supreme Court must, accordingly be reversed and the case remanded for further proceedings not inconsistent with this opinion. (*Id.* at 574-75)

Significance of the Decision. The decision in *Pickering* is definitely a "landmark decision" as far as legal rights of teachers are concerned. First of all, it should be realized, as the Court has frequently emphasized, that a classroom teacher is a citizen—and in that capacity has the right to speak, think, and believe as he wishes.

Admittedly, in expressing these rights as a citizen, the teacher must consider the effects upon others—particularly the school children. If Pickering's action could have been proved to be injurious to the pupil or disruptive to the educative process, it is unlikely that the Court would have ruled in his behalf.

In most of the court cases that have been discussed so far in this publication, the First Amendment rights of all citizens, including teachers, have entered into the Court's deliberations. That portion of the First Amendment directly applicable to *Pickering* is "freedom of speech."

The right for public school teachers to exercise their constitutional right of freedom of speech when participating in public affairs is usually held legal when done outside the classroom and during off-duty hours. An illustrative case (*Los Angeles Teachers Union* v. *Los Angeles City Board of Education*, 78 Cal. Rptr. 723, 1969) was litigated just one year after *Pickering* in which a somewhat similar issue was disposed of in a somewhat similar manner. Here a board regulation prohibiting teachers from circulating petitions concerning disputed budget proposals during off-duty hours was struck down by the Supreme Court of California.

Significantly, the language used by the California

court resembled that of the United States Supreme Court in *Pickering*:

> Teachers, like others, have the right to speak freely and effectively on public questions.... The government has no valid interest in restricting or prohibiting speech or speech-related activity simply in order to avert the sort of disturbance, argument or unrest which is inevitably generated by the expression of ideas which are controversial and invite dispute. The danger justifying restriction or prohibition must be one which rises above public inconvenience, annoyance, or unrest. This is so because the free expression of ideas concerning controversial matters is essential to our system of government. (*Id.* at 727-28)

Chapter 19

STATUTORY PROHIBITION TO TEACH THEORY OF EVOLUTION

(held unconstitutional)

Epperson v. *Arkansas*, 393
U.S. 97, 89 S. Ct. 266
(1968)

The Issue. Briefly stated, the issue in this case pertained to the constitutionality of an Arkansas "anti-evolution" law which prohibited the teaching in its public schools, the theory that man evolved from other species of life.

Background. The Arkansas statute, enacted in 1928, was an adaptation of the famous Tennessee "monkey law" of 1925—the constitutionality of which was upheld in 1927 by the Tennessee Supreme Court in the celebrated *Scopes* case. The Arkansas statute reads as follows:

> It shall be unlawful for any teacher or other instructor in any University, College, Normal, Public School, or other institution of the State, which is supported in whole or in part from public funds derived by State and local taxation to teach the theory or doctrine that mankind ascended or descended from a lower order of animals and also it shall be unlawful for any teacher, textbook commission, or other authority exercising the power to select textbooks for above-mentioned educational institutions to

> adopt or use in any such institution a
> textbook that teaches the doctrine or theory
> that mankind descended or ascended from a
> lower order of animals. (393 U.S. at 99)

As a consequence of the prohibitory nature of the
Arkansas law, the *Epperson* case was instituted in
the Chancery Court of the State by a teacher (Susan
Epperson) who sought a declaration that the statute
was void, and enjoined the State and defendant
officials from dismissing her for violation of the
statute which aimed to prohibit the teaching of
evolution. The Chancery Court, noting violation of
the statute with the "freedom of speech" clause of
the First Amendment, declared the statute to be
unconstitutional.

On appeal, the Supreme Court of Arkansas
reversed the decision of the Chancery Court,
claiming that the statute constituted "an exercise of
the State's power to specify the curriculum in public
schools." The State Supreme Court's ruling was then
appealed to the United States Supreme Court for
final jurisdiction.

U. S. Supreme Court Decision. In November of
1968, the United States Supreme Court reversed the
State Court decision and unanimously declared the
Arkansas statute to be unconstitutional on the
narrow grounds of the First Amendment's
"Establishment of Religion" clause.

Justice Fortas, who delivered the opinion of the
Court, stated:

> . . . the law must be stricken because of its
> conflict with the constitutional prohibition

of state laws respecting an establishment of religion or prohibiting the free exercise thereof. The overriding fact is that Arkansas' law selects from the body of knowledge a particular segment which it proscribes for the sole reason that it is deemed to conflict with a particular religious doctrine; that is, with a particular interpretation of the Book of Genesis by a particular religious group.

With reference to the State's general plenary power in the area of the curriculum, Justice Fortas emphasized that:

The State's undoubted right to prescribe the curriculum for its public schools does not carry with it the right to prohibit, on pain of criminal penalty, the teaching of a scientific theory or doctrine where that prohibition is based upon reasons that violate the First Amendment. It is much too late to argue that the State may impose upon the teachers in its schools any conditions that it chooses, however restrictive they may be of constitutional guarantees. . . .

In the present case, there can be no doubt that Arkansas has sought to prevent its teachers from discussing the theory of evolution because it is contrary to the belief of some that the Book of Genesis must be the exclusive source of doctrine as to the origin of man. No suggestion has been made that Arkansas' law may be justified by considerations of state policy other than the religious views of some of its citizens. It is clear that fundamentalist sectarian conviction was and is the law's reason for existence. Its antecedent, Tennessee's "monkey law" candidly stated its purpose: to make it unlawful "to teach any theory that denies the story of the Divine Creation of man as taught in the Bible, and to teach instead that man has descended from a lower order of animals." Perhaps the sensational publicity attendant upon the *Scopes* trial induced Arkansas to adopt less explicit language. It eliminated Tennessee's reference to "the story of the Divine Creation of man" as taught in the Bible, but there is no doubt that the motivation for the law was the same: to suppress the teaching of a theory which it was thought "denied" the divine creation of man.

Arkansas' law cannot be defended as an act of religious neutrality. Arkansas did not seek to excise from the curricula of its schools and universities all discussion of the origin of man. The law's effort was confined to an attempt to blot out a particular theory because of its supposed conflict with the Biblical account, literally read. Plainly, the law is contrary to the mandate of the First, and in violation of the Fourteenth, Amendment to the Constitution. (*Id.* at 107-9)

Justices Black and Stewart, although concurring in the unanimous decision, stressed opposition to the law because of its vagueness. Justice Black stated:

Under this statute as construed by the Arkansas Supreme Court, a teacher cannot know whether he is forbidden to mention Darwin's theory at all or only free to discuss it as long as he refrains from contending it is true. It is an established rule that a statute which leaves an ordinary man so doubtful about its meaning that he cannot know when he has violated it denies him the essential of due process. (*Id.* at 112)

Justice Stewart, in his concurring opinion, concluded his remarks as follows:

It is one thing for a State to determine that "the subject of higher mathematics, or astronomy, or biology" shall or shall not be included in its public school curriculum. It is quite another thing for a State to make it a criminal offense for a public school teacher so much as to mention the very existence of an entire system of respected human thought. That kind of criminal law, I think would clearly impinge upon the guarantee of free communication contained in the First Amendment, and made applicable to the States by the Fourteenth.

The Arkansas Supreme Court has said that the statute before us may or may not be just such a law. The result as Mr. Justice Black points out, is that "a teacher cannot know whether he is forbidden to mention Darwin's theory at all." Since I believe that no State could constitutionally forbid a teacher "to mention Darwin's theory at all," and since Arkansas may, or may not, have done just that, I conclude that the statute before us is so vague as to be invalid under the Fourteenth Amendment. (*Id.* at 116)

Significance of the Decision. Generally, the state has authority to determine the curricula for its school system. That authority, however, is not absolute. *Any state law which requires or prohibits the teaching of some matter that conflicts with the United States Constitution is void.* The Arkansas anti-evolution law provided a good example of this legal principle. It was unconstitutional for at least two reasons. First, it violated the Establishment of Religion Clause, and, second, it impinged upon the guarantee of free communication contained in the First Amendment.

For nearly a half century, legislators, school officials, teachers and parents had been in a quandry regarding the legality of having the theory of evolution (Darwinism) taught in the public schools. Several of the states in the "Bible Belt" (Arkansas, Mississippi and Tennessee) had had anti-evolution laws on their statute books for several decades—not knowing exactly the state of their constitutionality. All the doubt, however, was removed with the United States Supreme Court's decision in *Epperson.* Therefore state statutory provisions which were in conflict with *Epperson* have been repealed by the legislatures or nullified by the courts.

The last vestige was removed, in 1970, when the anti-evolution statute of Mississippi was invalidated by its Supreme Court. In this case (*Smith* v. *State,* 242 So. 2d 692 Miss. 1970) a prospective teacher challenged the statute on the grounds that she was being deprived of the opportunity "to gain a basic educational foundation from which she can receive the necessary technical, scientific training required to engage in the profession or business which depends upon scientific knowledge of anthropology and related subjects." (*Id.* at 694)

The State Supreme Court overruled a chancery court decision, and held—as did the United States Supreme Court earlier—that the anti-evolution statutes "are in contravention to the First Amendment to the Constitution of the United States." The State Supreme Court's decision was admittedly determined by the United States Supreme Court decision in the case of *Epperson.*

Chapter 20

STUDENTS' RIGHT TO EXPRESS SYMBOLIC OPPOSITION

(held constitutional)

Tinker v. *Des Moines Independent School District* (Ia.), 393 U.S. 503, 89 S. Ct. 733 (1969)

The Issue. In general, the question in this case is whether public-school students may express symbolic opposition to certain governmental activities. More directly, the issue concerned the legality of a school board policy banning the wearing of black armbands to symbolize and publicize objection to hostilities in Vietnam.

Background. Circumstances which prompted litigation in this case are described, in part, by the Court, as follows:

> Petitioner John F. Tinker, fifteen years old, and petitioner Christopher Eckhardt, sixteen years old, attended high schools in Des Moines, Iowa. Petitioner Mary Beth Tinker, John's sister, was a thirteen-year-old student in junior high school.
>
> In December 1965, a group of adults and students in Des Moines held a meeting at the Eckhardt home. The group determined to publicize their objections to the hostilities in Vietnam and their support for a truce by wearing black armbands during the holiday season and by fasting on December 16 and

New Year's Eve. Petitioners and their parents had previously engaged in similar activities, and they decided to participate in the program.

The principals of the Des Moines schools became aware of the plan to wear armbands. On December 14, 1965, they met and adopted a policy that any student wearing an armband to school would be asked to remove it, and if he refused he would be suspended until he returned without the armband. Petitioners were aware of the regulation that the school authorities adopted.

On December 16, Mary Beth and Christopher wore black armbands to their schools. John Tinker wore his armband the next day. They were all sent home and suspended from school until they would come back without their armbands. They did not return to school until after the planned period for wearing armbands had expired—that is, until after New Year's Day. (393 U.S. at 504)

Consequently the parents of the petitioners (pupils) filed a complaint in the United States District Court, praying for an injunction restraining the school administration and the school board from disciplining the offending pupils.

After an evidentiary hearing the District Court dismissed the complaint. It upheld the constitutionality of the school authorities' action on the ground that it was reasonable in order to prevent disturbance of school discipline.

On appeal the Court of Appeals for the Eighth

Circuit considered the case *en banc* and affirmed, without opinion, the decision of the District Court. Then, on further appeal, the case went to the United States Supreme Court for final settlement.

U. S. Supreme Court Decision. The United States Supreme Court *reversed* the decision of the Circuit Court and ruled that the wearing of armbands, as done in the Des Moines situation was a constitutional right guaranteed by the First Amendment.

Justice Fortas, who delivered the opinion of the Court, pointed out that:

> First Amendment rights, applied in light of the special characteristics of the school environment, are available to teachers and students. It can hardly be argued that either students or teachers shed their constitutional right to freedom of speech or expression at the schoolhouse gate. This has been the unmistakable holding of this Court for almost 50 years. (*Id.* at 506)

The High Court disagreed with the contentions of the District Court that the school's ban on wearing the armbands was "reasonable in order to prevent disturbance of school discipline." In this connection, the Supreme Court made a lengthy denial as follows:

> The school officials banned and sought to punish petitioners for a silent, passive expression of opinion, unaccompanied by any disorder or disturbance on the part of petitioners. There is no evidence whatever of petitioners' interference, actual or nascent, with the schools' work or of collision with the rights of other students to

be secure and be let alone. Accordingly, this case does not concern speech or action that intrudes upon the work of the schools or the rights of other students.

Only a few of the 18,000 students in the school system wore the black armbands. Only five students were suspended for wearing them. There is no indication that the work of the schools or any class was disrupted. Outside the classrooms, a few students made hostile remarks to the children wearing armbands; but there were no threats or acts of violence on school premises.

The District Court concluded that the action of the school authorities was reasonable because it was based upon their fear of a disturbance from the wearing of the armbands. But, in our system, undifferentiated fear or apprehension of disturbance is not enough to overcome the right to freedom of expression. Any departure from absolute regimentation may cause trouble. Any variation from the majority's opinion may inspire fear. Any word spoken, in class, in the lunchroom, or on the campus, that deviates from the views of another person may start an argument or cause a disturbance. But our Constitution says we must take this risk; and our history says that it is this sort of hazardous freedom—this kind of openness—that is the basis of our national strength and the independence and vigor of Americans who grow up and live in this relatively permissive, often disputatious society.

In order for the State in the person of

school officials to justify prohibition of a particular expression of opinion, it must be able to show that its action was caused by something more than a mere desire to avoid the discomfort and unpleasantness that always accompany an unpopular viewpoint. Certainly where there is no finding and no showing that engaging in the forbidden conduct would materially and substantially interfere with the requirements of appropriate discipline in the operation of the school, the prohibition cannot be sustained. (*Id.* at 508-9)

In our system, state-operated schools may not be enclaves of totalitarianism. School officials do not possess absolute authority over their students. Students in school as well as out of school are "persons" under our Constitution. They are possessed of fundamental rights which the State must respect, just as they themselves must respect their obligation to the State. In our system, students may not be regarded as closed-circuit recipients of only that which the State chooses to communicate. They may not be confined to the expression of those sentiments that are officially approved. In the absence of a specific showing as constitutionally valid reasons to regulate their speech, students are entitled to freedom of expression of their views. (*Id.* at 511)

Justice Black took sharp issue with the opinion of the majority. In the opening paragraph of his bitter dissent he stated: "The Court's holding in this case ushers in what I deem to be an entirely new era in which the power to control pupils by the elected 'officials of state supported public schools . . .' in the United States is in ultimate effect transferred to the Supreme Court." (*Id.* at 515)

By way of concluding his dissent, Justice Black vigorously remarked:

> One does not need to be a prophet or the son of a prophet to know that after the Court's holding today some students in Iowa schools and indeed in all schools will be ready, able, and willing to defy their teachers on practically all orders. This is the more unfortunate for the schools since groups of students all over the land are already running loose, conducting break-ins, sit-ins, lie-ins, and smash-ins. Many of these student groups, as is all too familiar to all who read the newspapers and watch the television news programs, have already engaged in rioting, property seizures, and destruction. They have picketed schools to force students not to cross their picket lines and have too often violently attacked earnest but frightened students who wanted an education that the pickets did not want them to get. Students engaged in such activities are apparently confident that they know far more about how to operate public school systems than do their parents, teachers, and elected school officials. It is no answer to say that the particular students here have not yet reached such high points in their demands to attend classes in order to exercise their political pressures. Turned loose with lawsuits for damages and injunctions against their teachers as they

are here, it is nothing but wishful thinking to imagine that young, immature students will not soon believe it is their right to control the schools rather than the right of the States that collect the taxes to hire the teachers for the benefit of the pupils. This case, therefore, wholly without con-stitutional reasons in my judgment, subjects all the public schools in the country to the whims and caprices of their loudest-mouthed, but maybe not their brightest students. I, for one, am not fully persuaded that school pupils are wise enough, even with this Court's expert help from Washington, to run the 23,390 public school systems in our 50 states. I wish, therefore, wholly to disclaim any purpose on my part to hold that the Federal Constitution compels the teachers, parents, and elected school officials to surrender control of the American public school system to public school students. I dissent. (*Id.* at 525-26)

Significance of the Decision. The Supreme Court emphasized that the wearing of armbands was a constitutional right of expression guaranteed by the First Amendment. *All citizens* enjoy this guarantee of the Constitution. Therefore it is not denied to students in the public schools. As the Court stated: "It can hardly be argued that either students or teachers shed their constitutional rights to freedom of speech or expression at the schoolhouse gate."

The right of expression, however, is not absolute. When it can be proved that the symbolic expression is conducive to disruptive and injurious classroom discipline and decorum, the activity is not judicially condoned. But mere fear or apprehension of the disturbance is not sufficient reason for a school board to take away the constitutional right of freedom of speech. Despite the prophetic nature of the warning in Justice Black's dissenting opinion, the Court found no evidence in the *Tinker* case that actual harm to the school resulted from the wearing of the armbands.

The wearing of armbands or any other strategem of symbolic expression, such as wearing long hair or display of "freedom buttons," may or may not be within constitutional limits. Two federal court cases on the wearing of buttons illustrate the demarcation between permissible and impermissible practice.

In the first case (*Burnside* v. *Byars* (Miss.), 363 F.2d 744, 1966) the Court *invalidated* a school regulation to prohibit the wearing of freedom buttons because in so doing it "did not hamper the school in carrying on its regular schedule of activities; nor would it seem likely that the simple wearing of buttons unaccompanied by improper conduct would even do so." (*Id.* at 747)

In a companion case (*Blackwell* v. *Issaquena County Board of Education* (Miss.), 363 F.2d 749, 1966) decided by the same court on the same day, the issue was the same—a civil rights action to enjoin school officials from enforcing a regulation forbidding the wearing of freedom buttons. Because of markedly different circumstances, however, the Court *validated* the board prohibitive regulation. Here "students conducted themselves in a disorderly manner, disrupted classroom procedure, interfered with the proper decorum and discipline of the school and disturbed other students who did not wish to participate in the wearing of the buttons." (*Id.* at 753)

Likewise, in a more recent case (*Hill* v. *Lewis* (N.C.), 323 F. Supp. 55, 1971), unlike that of *Tinker*, students in a North Carolina high school were *not* permitted to wear armbands (which were black, red, white and blue) to symbolize diverse factions with respect to war and nonwar issues. The United States District Court, after finding evidence of undue interference with the school program, concluded its support of the board ruling by stating:

In the balancing of First Amendment rights the duty of the State to operate its public school system for the benefit of *all* its children must be protected even if governmental regulations incidentally limit the untrammeled exercise of speech, symbolic or otherwise, by those who would impede the education of those who desire to learn. The interest of the State is superior to the rights of the protestants." (*Id.* at 59)

Chapter 21

ALLOCATION OF PUBLIC FUNDS FOR NON-PUBLIC SCHOOLS

(held unconstitutional)

Lemon v. *Kurtzman* (Pa.);
Earley v. *Di Censo* (R.I.),
403 U.S. 602, 91 S. Ct.
2105 (1971)

The Issue. The issue in these companion cases concerned the constitutionality of state aid to, or for the benefit of non-public schools. Two state programs were at issue. The Rhode Island program pertained to salary supplements paid to teachers of secular subjects in non-public schools. The Pennsylvania program involved reimbursement to non-public schools for teachers' salaries, textbooks, and instructional materials used in the teaching of specific secular subjects.

Background. For many decades and in many states there had been litigation concerning statutory provisions for indirect aid to parochial schools at public expense. In 1930, the issue reached the United States Supreme Court in the 1930 *Cochran* textbook case, *supra.* Then again, in 1947, the Court ruled on the *Everson* pupil transportation case, *supra.* In both instances the Supreme Court validated the constitutionality of the *indirect* aid to non-public schools.

Following those decisions, numerous attempts have been made toward attaining more *direct* aid for non-public schools at public expense. The issue finally reached a climax in 1971 when the constitutionality of direct state aid to non-public schools was carried to the United States Supreme Court for a ruling concerning the Rhode Island Act of 1969 which "authorizes state officials to supplement the salaries of teachers of secular subjects in non-public elementary schools by paying directly to a teacher an amount not in excess of 15% of his current annual salary." Also, the Pennsylvania Non-public Elementary and Secondary Education Act of 1968 "authorizes the State Superintendent of Public Instruction to purchase certain secular educational services from non-public schools, directly reimbursing those schools solely for teachers' salaries, textbooks, and instructional materials."

Following actions challenging the constitutionality of these Acts, a Federal District Court concluded that the Rhode Island Act "violated the Establishment Clause," holding that it fostered "excessive entanglement" between government and religion. In addition two judges thought that the Act had the impermissible effect of giving "significant aid to a religious enterprise."

However, in the Pennsylvania case, a lower federal court dismissed the complaint and held that "the Act violated neither the Establishment nor the Free Exercise Clause." Both decisions were then appealed to the United States Supreme Court.

U. S. Supreme Court Decision. The United States Supreme Court, with Chief Justice Burger delivering the opinion, affirmed the judgment of the lower court on the Rhode Island Act, but reversed that of the lower court on the Pennsylvania Act. In consequence, the United States Supreme Court "held that both statutes were unconstitutional under the religious clauses of the First Amendment, though promoting secular legislative purposes, since both involved excessive entanglement of state with church."

The Supreme Court agreed, in abstract, with the contentions of the legislatures of Rhode Island and Pennsylvania that "secular and religious education are identifiable and separable" but reasoned that:

> The two legislatures, however, have also recognized that church-related elementary and secondary schools have a significant religious mission and that a substantial portion of their activities are religiously oriented. They have therefore sought to create statutory restrictions designed to guarantee the separation between secular and religious educational functions and to ensure that State financial aid supports only the former. All these provisions are precautions taken in candid recognition that these programs approached, even if they did not intrude upon the forbidden areas under the Religion Clauses. We need not decide whether these legislative precautions restrict the principal or primary effect of the programs to the point where they do not offend the Religion Clauses, for we conclude that the cumulative impact of the entire relationship arising under the statutes in each State involves excessive entanglements

between government and religion. (403 U.S.
at 613-14)

A difficulty in keeping religious instruction and
secular instruction separable is pointed out by the
Court in the following passage:

> We need not and do not assume that
> teachers in parochial schools will be guilty
> of bad faith or any conscious design to evade
> the limitations imposed by the statute and
> the First Amendment. We simply recognize
> that a dedicated religious person, teaching
> in a school affiliated with his or her faith
> and operated to inculcate its tenets, will
> inevitably experience great difficulty in
> remaining religiously neutral. Doctrines
> and faith are not inculcated or advanced by
> neutrals. With the best of intentions such a
> teacher would find it hard to make a total
> separation between secular teaching and
> religious doctrine. What would appear to
> some to be essential to good citizenship
> might well for others border on or constitute
> instruction in religion. Further difficulties
> are inherent in the combination of religious
> discipline   and   the   possibility   of   dis-
> agreement between teacher and religious
> authorities   over   the   meaning   of   the
> statutory restrictions.

> We   do   not   assume,   however,   that
> parochial   school   teachers   will   be   un-
> successful in their attempts to segregate
> their religious beliefs from their secular
> educational   responsibilities.   But   the
> potential for impermissible fostering of
> religion is present. The Rhode Island
> Legislature has not, and could not, provide

state aid on the basis of a mere assumption that secular teachers under religious discipline can avoid conflicts. The State must be certain, given the Religious Clauses, that subsidized teachers do not inculcate religion. . . . (*Id.* at 618-19)

Chief Justice Burger finalized the Court's opinion with the following passage:

Finally, nothing we have said can be construed to disparage the role of church-related elementary and secondary schools in our national life. Their contributions have been and are enormous. Nor do we ignore their economic plight in a period of rising costs and expanding need. Taxpayers generally have been spared vast sums by the maintenance of these educational institutions by religious organizations, largely by the gifts of faithful adherents.

The merit and benefits of these schools, however, are not the issue before us in these cases. The sole question is whether state aid to these schools can be squared with the dictates of the Religious Clauses. Under our system the choice has been made that government is to be entirely excluded from the area of religious instruction and churches excluded from the affairs of government. The Constitution decrees that religion must be a private matter for the individual, the family, and the institutions, of private choice, and that while some involvement and entanglement is inevitable, lines must be drawn. (*Id.* at 624-25)

In a concurring opinion, Justice Douglas, joined by

Justice Black, reiterated the sentiments expressed in the majority opinion, as indicated by the following concise statement:

> If the government closed its eyes to the manner in which these grants are actually used it would be allowing public funds to promote sectarian education. If it did not close its eyes but undertook the surveillance needed, it would, I fear, intermeddle in parochial affairs in a way that would breed only rancor and dissention.
> We have announced over and over again that the use of taxpayers' money to support parochial schools violates the First Amendment, applicable to the States by virtue of the Fourteenth. (*Id.* at 640)

Significance of the Decision. One end of the wall separating church and state had been fortified by judicial rulings; whereas, the other end had been gradually eroding.

Decisions in *Engel* v. *Vitale* and *Abington* v. *Schempp*, *supra*, exemplify where the wall has been fortified. The Court's invalidation of religious influences in the public schools, such as Bible reading and the recitation of prayers, placed a definite restriction on religious exercises in the public schools. Subsequent cases on the issue of religious instruction in the public schools have been decided in conformity with the restrictive precedent established by *Engel* and *Schempp*.

However, Supreme Court decisions in the earlier cases, *Cochran* and *Everson*, *supra*, indicate a gradual erosion at the other end of the wall, by means of what is referred to as "parochiaid." The Court's validation of supplying free textbooks and transportation to parochial pupils at public expense, under the "child benefit" theory has triggered legislative enactments to supply other materials and services to parochial pupils at public expense. At present there are approximately eighty laws on the statute books in various states for public assistance to parochial schools or parochial pupils.

Such *indirect* aid, however, has not been sufficient to get the parochial schools (Catholic) out of their financial difficulties. Consequently. attempts have been made to secure *direct* public aid to the parochial schools. The decisions of *Lemon* and *Kurtzman* and its companion case have brought an abrupt cessation of that type of parochiaid. So a firm wall separating church and state has been restored at both ends.

As has been reported above, the statutes in Pennsylvania and Rhode Island were declared unconstitutional because they involved "excessive entanglement of state with church." Consequently, hereafter, any parochial aid—whether direct or indirect—will be measured against a strict construction of the United States Constitution pertaining to the Establishment Clause of the First Amendment.

For example, on January 11, 1972, a three-judge federal court struck down a New York statute designed to provide $33 million in state aid for non-public schools during the current year. As was the case in *Lemon* v. *Kurtzman* the Court based its decision on the Establishment of Religion Clause contained in the First Amendment.

As a consequence of judicial restrictions on parochiaid, the President of the United States, and others, are attempting to ease the financial burden of the non-public schools by other forms of subsidy or reimbursement, such as voucher programs or tax credits. In the event legislation is enacted for such purposes, its constitutionality will likely be tested in the courts as was *Lemon v. Kurtzman.*

That the legal principle laid down in *Lemon* will be applied to other cases where direct aid for non-public schools is sought, is evidenced in the 1972 Ohio case (*Wolman* v. *Essex*, 342 F. Supp. 399, 1972). Here certain portions of an Ohio statute authorized grants to reimburse parents of non-public school children for a portion of tuition paid by them. A three-judge District Court held the statute violated the "establishment clause." In pointing out an infirmity of the statute, the Court stated, in part:

> As noted earlier, the Supreme Court has been highly suspicious of subsidy programs, as evidenced by the warning in *Lemon* that subsidies tend to foment "political fragmentation and divisiveness on religious lines." Whereas direct money subsidies promote the same general construction grants, the risks of political entanglement attendant upon them are far greater. (*Id.* at 417)

Chapter 22

BUSING OF STUDENTS TO ACHIEVE RACIAL BALANCE

(held constitutional)

Swann v. *Charlotte-Mecklenburg Board of Education* (N.C.), 402 U.S. 1, 91 S. Ct. 1267 (1971)

The Issue. The general issue in this case is that of student assignment. Specifically the issue is whether busing of students is a legitimate means of assignment and a constitutional desegregation tool to dismantle the dual school system.

Background. The Charlotte-Mecklenburg school system, like many other school systems in the South, was confronted with the problem of implementing the *Brown* decisions and the judicial mandate to eliminate dual systems and to establish unitary systems.

Two United States Supreme Court decisions, (*Green* v. *County School Board* (Va.), 391 U.S. 430, 88 S. Ct. 1689, 1968) and *Alexander* v. *Holmes County Board of Education* (Miss.), 396 U.S. 19, 90 S. Ct. 14, 1969, hastened school systems to employ and experiment with "busing" as a means of eliminating dual systems. While acknowledging that a freedom-of-choice concept could be a valid remedial measure in some circumstances, its failure to be effective in *Green* required that "The burden on a school board today is to come forward with a plan that promises realistically to work now. . . . Moreover, whatever plan is adopted will require evaluation in practice, and the court should retain jurisdiction until it is clear that state-imposed segregation has been completely removed." (*Green*, 391 U.S. at 439).

And, noting in *Alexander* v. *Holmes* that "gradualism" which had been permitted by lower federal courts, the Supreme Court ordered that: "Under explicit holdings of the Court the obligation of every school district is to terminate dual school systems at once and to operate now and hereafter only unitary schools." (396 U.S. at 20, 1969).

Mandates, such as these, prompted school districts to comply by experimenting with various tools of desegregation—including the busing of students.

The "Syllabus" which prefaces the Court's opinion describes, as follows, the situation as it existed in the 1968-69 school year and carried through 1970:

> The Charlotte-Mecklenburg school system, which includes the city of Charlotte, North Carolina, had more than 84,000 students in 107 schools in the 1968-1969 school year. Approximately 29% (24,000) of the pupils were Negro, about 14,000 of whom attended 21 schools that were at least 99% Negro. This resulted from a desegregation plan approved by the District Court in 1965, at the commencement of the litigation. In 1968 petitioner Swann moved for further relief based on *Green* v. *County School Board, supra,* which required school boards to "come forward with a plan that promises realistically to work . . . *now* . . . until it is clear that state-imposed

segregation has been completely removed."
The District Court ordered the school board
in April 1969 to provide a plan for faculty
and student desegregation. Finding the
board's submission unsatisfactory, the
District Court appointed an expert to
submit a desegregation plan. In February
1970, the expert and the board presented
plans, and the court adopted the board's
plan, as modified, for the junior and senior
high schools, and the expert's proposed plan
for the elementary schools. The Court of
Appeals affirmed the District Court's order
as to faculty desegregation and the
secondary school plans, but vacated the
order respecting elementary schools,
fearing that the provisions for pairing and
grouping of elementary schools would
unreasonably burden the pupils and the
board. The case was remanded to the
District Court for reconsideration and
submission of further plans. The Court
granted certiorari and directed rein-
statement of the District Court's order
pending further proceedings in that court.
On remand the District Court received two
new plans, and ordered the board to adopt a
plan, or the expert's plan would remain in
effect. After the board "acquiesced" in the
expert's plan, the District Court directed
that it remain in effect. (402 U.S. at 1-2)

U. S. Supreme Court Decision. On April 20, 1971,
the United States Supreme Court, with Chief Justice
Burger writing the opinion, unanimously upheld the
constitutionality of busing students to "dismantle
the dual school systems" of the South, but made it

clear that the decision did not apply to Northern style segregation, based on neighborhood patterns.

The Court spoke at length on the federal court's authority and responsibility in the framing of equitable remedies to repair the denial of a constitutional right. In this connection the Court stated:

> In seeking to define even in broad and general terms how far this remedial power extends it is important to remember that judicial powers may be exercised only on the basis of a constitutional violation. Remedial judicial authority does not put judges automatically in the shoes of school authorities whose powers are plenary. Judicial authority enters only when local authority defaults.
>
> School authorities are traditionally charged with broad power to formulate and implement educational policy and might well conclude, for example, that in order to prepare students to live in a pluralistic society each school should have a prescribed ratio of Negro to white students reflecting the proportion for the district as a whole. To do this as an educational policy is within the broad discretionary powers of school authorities; absent a finding of a constitutional violation, however, that would not be within the authority of a federal court. As with any equity case, the nature of the violation determines the scope of the remedy. In default by the school authorities of their obligation to proffer acceptable remedies, a district court has

broad power to fashion a remedy that will assure a unitary school system.

The school authorities argue that the equity powers of federal district courts have been limited by Title IV of the Civil Rights Act of 1964. The language and history of Title IV show that it was not enacted to limit but to define the role of the Federal Government in the implementation of the *Brown I* decision. It authorizes the Commissioner of Education to provide technical assistance to local boards in the preparation of desegregation plans, to arrange "training institutes" for school personnel involved in desegregation efforts, and to make grants directly to schools to ease the transition to unitary systems. It also authorizes the Attorney General, in specified circumstances, to initiate federal desegregation suits. . . .

There is no suggestion of an intention to restrict those powers or withdraw from courts their historic equitable remedial powers. The legislative history of Title IV indicates that Congress was concerned that the Act might be read as creating a right of action under the Fourteenth Amendment in the situation of so-called "de facto segregation," where racial imbalance exists in the schools but with no showing that this was brought about by discriminatory action of state authorities. In short, there is nothing in the Act which provides us material assistance in answering the question of remedy for state-imposed segregation in violation of *Brown I*. The basis of our decision must be the prohibition of the Fourteenth Amendment that no State shall "deny to any person within its jurisdiction the equal protection of the laws." (*Id.* at 16-18)

The Court elucidated on four problem areas existing on the issue of student assignment: (1) racial balances or racial quotas, (2) one-race schools, (3) remedial altering of attendance zones, and (4) transportation of students.

Since "transportation of students" involves "busing" and is the main area of contention in this case, the Court's concluding comments on it are quoted as follows:

> The scope of permissible transportation of students as an implement of a remedial decree has never been defined by this Court and by the very nature of the problem it cannot be defined with precision. No rigid guidelines as to student transportation can be given for application to the infinite variety of problems presented in thousands of situations. Bus transportation has been an integral part of the public education system for years, and was perhaps the single most important factor in the transition from the one-room schoolhouse to the consolidated school. Eighteen million of the Nation's public school children, approximately 39%, were transported to their schools by bus in 1969-1970 in all parts of the country.
>
> The importance of bus transportation as a normal and accepted tool of the educational policy is readily discernible in this and the companion case, *Davis, supra.* The

Charlotte school authorities did not purport to assign students on the basis of geographically drawn zones until 1965 and then they allowed almost unlimited transfer privileges. The District Court's conclusion that assignment of children to the school nearest their home serving their grade would not produce an effective dismantling of the dual system is supported by the record.

Thus the remedial techniques used in the District Court's order were within that court's power to provide equitable relief; implementation of the decree is well within the capacity of the school authority.

The decree provided that the buses used to implement the plan would operate on direct routes. Students would be picked up at schools near their homes and transported to the schools they were to attend. The trips for elementary school pupils average about seven miles and the District Court found that they would take "not over 35 minutes at the most." This system compares favorably with the transportation plan previously operated in Charlotte under which each day 23,600 students on all grade levels were transported an average of 15 miles one way for an average trip requiring over an hour. In these circumstances, we find no basis for holding that the local school authorities may not be required to employ bus transportation as one tool of school desegregation. Desegregation plans cannot be limited to the walk-in school.

An objection to transportation of students may have validity when the time or distance of travel is so great as to either risk the health of the children or significantly impinge on the educational process. District courts must weigh the soundness of any transportation plan in light of what is said in subdivisions (1), (2), and (3) above. It hardly needs stating that the limits on time of travel will vary with many factors, but probably with none more than age of the students. The reconciliation of competing values in a desegregation case is, of course, a difficult task with many sensitive facets but fundamentally no more so than remedial measures courts of equity have traditionally employed. (*Id.* at 29-31)

Significance of the Decision. It was to be expected that the decision in *Brown* would trigger more litigation on the issue of racial desegregation in the public schools. And so it did. A multitude of cases related to the issue have been decided in the lower federal courts, as well as several in the United States Supreme Court. None, however, has caused more public concern than the *Swann* decision. In fact there appears to be more public reaction, in the way of opposition, frustration, and emotion, or the issue of busing than there was on the *Brown* decision in 1954.

One reason was that the mandates in the *Brown* decision were comparatively conservative—allowing for "gradualism" to be employed in doing away with the dual system. In *Swann*, however, school districts were ordered to dismantle the dual systems *immediately* and *completely* by employing such tools as are necessary—including the busing of students—to achieve racial balances. "Prompt speed" rather than "deliberate speed" was the password.

Also, the fact that the issue of busing students was injected into the political campaigns in 1972, emotional reactions were aggravated. Certain candidates characterized busing of students as "asinine" and "senseless" and promised to do away with it by urging congressional action or an amendment to the federal constitution.

Although the White House called upon the American people, following the decision, to obey the ruling that mass busing is a legitimate tool to desegregate public schools, later attitudes have not been conducive to the support of the Court's unanimous decision. President Nixon's antibusing views have been given a great deal of publicity. He has requested a moratorium on federal court-ordered busing, and asked Congress to forbid courts to prescribe busing during the moratorium while some other means of providing equal educational opportunities are being sought. He has also hinted, as have other public officials, that as a last resort he would consider an enactment for amendment to the federal constitution.

Many legal experts express doubts that congressional interference with the Court's decision or the proposed amendment to the Constitution would be wise or constitutional. Aside from the constitutionality of the proposals, there is concern by many that their adoption would seriously interfere with the judicial branch of our federal government. The Founding Fathers never intended that either the executive branch or the legislative branch could invade the prerogative of a coequal branch of government—the judiciary.

Even if congressional action or amendment to the Constitution could legally impede massive busing such as allowed in *Swann*, the public reaction would be disastrous. The divisiveness between those who approve or disapprove massive busing to insure unitary school systems would become much more acute.

Chapter 23

COMPULSORY SCHOOL ATTENDANCE OF AMISH CHILDREN

(held unconstitutional)

Wisconsin v. *Yoder*, 49 Wis. 2d 430, 92 S. Ct. 1526 (1972)

The Issue. The issue here concerns the validity of the State's compulsory school attendance law which requires children, between the ages of seven and sixteen years, to attend a public or private school. The specific constitutional question is whether Amish parents are exempt from the law under the Free Exercise Clause of the First Amendment to the Constitution because of their conflicting religious beliefs.

Background. Litigation on the issue is not new. Amish parents in a number of states have repeatedly been called into the courts and jailed or fined for refusing to comply with compulsory school attendance laws. This is the first time, however, that the issue has reached the United States Supreme Court.

The litigation in this case had its beginning in September of 1968, when Jonas Yoder and Adin Yutzy, who are members of the Old Order Amish Religion, were convicted for violating Wisconsin's compulsory school attendance law (which requires a child's school attendance until age sixteen) by declining to send their children to a public or private school after they had graduated from the eighth grade. (They did not object to elementary education.) In defense of their noncompliance with the law, the Amish parents insisted that high school attendance is contrary to the Amish religion and way of life and that they "endanger their own salvation and that of their children by complying with the law."

A trial court denied a motion to dismiss the charges because it did not consider the Wisconsin compulsory school attendance law interfered with the freedoms of parents and children to act in accordance with their religious beliefs and that, therefore, the law was a "reasonable and constitutional" exercise of governmental power.

The Wisconsin Circuit Court affirmed the decision of the trial court and the convictions. On appeal, however, the State Supreme Court reversed the rulings of the lower courts and sustained the Amish parents' claim under the Free Exercise Clause of the First Amendment.

In reviewing the case (*State* v. *Yoder*, 49 Wis. 2d 430, 182 N.W.2d 539, 1971) the Supreme Court of Wisconsin minimized the effect of exemption to the compulsory attendance law in this particular case as indicated by the following statements:

> "Granting an exemption from compulsory education to the Amish will do no more to the ultimate goal of education than to dent the symmetry of the design for enforcement." (182 N.W.2d at 545)

> "We conclude that although education is a subject within the constitutional power of

the state to regulate, there is not such a compelling state interest in two years high school compulsory education as will justify the burden it places upon appellants' free exercise of their religion." (*Id.* at 547)

U. S. Supreme Court Decision. With Chief Justice Burger delivering the opinion, the United States Supreme Court affirmed the decision of the Wisconsin Supreme Court—holding that the First and Fourteenth Amendments prevent a state from compelling Amish parents to cause their children, who have graduated from the eighth grade, to attend formal high school to age sixteen.

The Court showed respect and support for the Amish religious principles as described in testimony by experts of Amish society:

Amish objection to formal education beyond the eighth grade is firmly grounded in these central religious concepts. They object to the high school and higher education generally because the values it teaches are in marked variance with Amish values and the Amish way of life; they view secondary school education as an impermissible exposure of their children to a "worldly" influence in conflict with their beliefs. The high school tends to emphasize intellectual and scientific accomplishments, self-distinction, competitiveness, worldly success, and social life with other students. Amish society emphasizes informal learning-through-doing, a life of "goodness," rather than a life of intellect, wisdom, rather than technical knowledge, community welfare rather than competition, and separation, rather than integration with contemporary worldly society.

Formal high school education beyond the eighth grade is contrary to Amish beliefs not only because it places Amish children in an environment hostile to Amish beliefs with increasing emphasis on competition in class work and sports and with pressure to conform to the styles, manners and ways of the peer group, but because it takes them away from their community, physically and emotionally, during the crucial and formative adolescent period of life. During this period the children must acquire Amish attitudes favoring manual work and self-reliance and the specific skills needed to perform the adult role of an Amish farmer or housewife. They must learn to enjoy physical labor. Once a child has learned basic reading, writing, and elementary mathematics, these traits, skills, and attitudes admittedly fall within the category of those best learned through example and "doing" rather than in a classroom. And, at this time in life, the Amish child must also grow in his faith and relationship to the Amish community if he is to be prepared to accept the heavy obligations imposed by adult baptism. In short, high school attendance with teachers who are not of the Amish faith—and may even be hostile to it—interposes a serious barrier to the integration of the Amish child into the Amish religious community. (92 S. Ct. at 1531)

The record shows that the respondents' religious beliefs and attitude toward life, family, and home have remained constant—perhaps some would say static—in a period of unparalleled progress in human knowledge generally and great changes in education. The respondents freely concede, and indeed assert as an article of faith, that their religious beliefs and what we today would call "life style" has not altered in fundamentals for centuries. Their way of life in a church-oriented community, separated from the outside world and "worldly" influences, their attachment to nature and the soil, is a way inherently simple and uncomplicated, albeit difficult to preserve against the pressure to conform. Their rejection of telephones, automobiles, radios, and television, their mode of dress, of speech, their habits of manual work do indeed set them apart from much of contemporary society; these customs are both symbolic and practical. (*Id.* at 1534)

In sum, the unchallenged testimony of acknowledged experts in education and religious history, almost 300 years of consistent practice, and strong evidence of a sustained faith pervading and regulating respondents' entire mode of life support the claim that enforcement of the State's requirement of compulsory formal education after the eighth grade would gravely endanger if not destroy the free exercise of respondents' religious beliefs. (*Id.* at 1535)

The Court stressed that it was not assuming the role of school boards or legislatures in determining a

State's program of compulsory education, and suggested "that courts must move with great circumspection in performing the sensitive and delicate task of weighing a State's legitimate social concern when faced with religious claims for exemption from generally applicable educational requirements."

Realizing that the Court's decision might encourage other religious groups to violate compulsory school attendance laws because of alleged religious conflicts, the Court indicated the decision was applicable only to the Amish because of their proven sincerity in the educational requirement believed to be in conformity with their religious views. In this respect the Court concluded with the following comment:

> Aided by a history of three centuries as an identifiable religious sect and a long history as a successful and self-sufficient segment of American society, the Amish in this case have convincingly demonstrated the sincerity of their religious beliefs, the interrelationship of belief with their mode of life, the vital role which belief and daily conduct play in the continued survival of Old Order Amish communities and their religious organization, and the hazards presented by the State's enforcement of a statute generally valid as to others. Beyond this, they have carried the even more difficult burden of demonstrating the adequacy of their alternative mode of continuing informal vocational education in terms of precisely those overall interests that the State advances in support of its

program of compulsory high school education. In light of this convincing showing, one which probably few other religious groups or sects could make, and weighing the minimal difference between what the states would require and what the Amish already accept, it was incumbent on the State to show with more particularity how its admittedly strong interest in compulsory education would be adversely affected by granting an exemption to the Amish. (*Id.* at 1543)

Justices Powell and Rehnquist took no part in the consideration or decision of the case; Justice Stewart, with whom Justice Brennan joined, concurred and filed an opinion; Justice White, with whom Justices Brennan and Stewart joined, concurred and filed an opinion; Justice Douglas dissented, in part, and filed an opinion.

Although Justice Douglas agreed with the Court that the religious scruples of the Amish are opposed to the education of their children beyond the grade schools, he disagreed with the Court's conclusion that the matter is within the dispensation of parents alone.

Since a significant number of Amish children leave the Old Order, Justice Douglas is concerned with the possible handicaps such children might encounter outside the Amish community. He, therefore, expresses his belief that the child should have a voice in his educational future. The main thrust of Justice Douglas's dissent is depicted in the following passage:

On this important and vital matter of

education, I think the children should be entitled to be heard. While the parents, absent dissent, normally speak for the entire family, the education of the child is a matter on which the child will often have decided views. He may want to be a pianist or an astronaut or an ocean geographer. To do so he will have to break from the Amish tradition.

It is the future of the student, not the future of the parents, that is imperilled in today's decision. If a parent keeps his child out of school beyond the grade school, then the child will be forever barred from entry into the new and amazing world of diversity that we have today. The child may decide that that is the preferred course, or he may rebel. It is the student's judgment, not his parents, that is essential if we are to give full meaning to what we have said about the Bill of Rights and of the right of students to be masters of their own destiny. If he is harnessed to the Amish way of life by those in authority over him and if his education is truncated, his entire life may be stunted and deformed. The child, therefore, should be given an opportunity to be heard before the State gives the exemption which we honor today. (*Id.* at 1547-48)

Significance of the Decision. The legality and propriety of compulsory school attendance has been viewed differently through the various periods of public education. At first compulsory school attendance was opposed by reason of the common law which authorized absolute parental control over the child's education. Later the public—and especially the judiciary—rejected this common law principle because of its possible deprivation of the child's welfare as well as that of society. Consequently compulsory school attendance laws were passed, which, at first, were challenged because they interfered with the natural rights of parents to control the welfare of their children. Despite some judicial vacillation over the issue, the courts eventually became consistent in ruling that the state had sufficient power to enact and enforce compulsory school attendance legislation.

The earlier laws required that the attendance would be in public schools only. However, as early as 1925 (*Pierce, supra*) such laws were declared unconstitutional, and non-public schooling was accepted as an alternative, if meeting required educational standards. Then later, home instruction, in lieu of school instruction, was sanctioned, providing the home instruction was equivalent to that which would be obtainable in a public school. Now, in the light of *Yoder*, it appears that home instruction need not be equivalent or similar to that provided in a public school when certain constitutional provisions are involved.

The decision in *Yoder* indicates that compulsory school attendance laws will not be upheld when they impinge on fundamental rights and interests, such as those protected by the free exercise clause of the First Amendment and the traditional interest of parents with respect to religious upbringing of their children.

A possible consequence of the *Yoder* decision is

that members of other religious sects might attempt noncompliance with compulsory school attendance requirements because of conflicts with their alleged religious scruples. It is not likely, however, that they could convince a court that their conflicting religious beliefs were of such magnitude as would justify exemption from compulsory school attendance requirements. Moreover, it is not likely that any other religious group could develop a home educational program, in lieu of public education, that would be as sufficient as that provided by the Amish.

In some respects the post elementary education provided by the Amish is considered superior to that provided in many of our high schools today. At least it fits them better for the lives they live in the Amish community than what they would receive in a typical public high school. Of course, for those who leave the Amish community the education received there may be—as feared by Justice Douglas—lacking for life in the general society.

The decision in *Yoder* is comforting to those whose views and dress are not in conformity with those of the majority. As the Court expressed: "A way of life that is odd or even erratic but interferes with the rights and interests of others is not to be condemned because it is different."

Chapter 24

ALTERATION OF SCHOOL DISTRICT BOUNDARIES TO AVOID COMPLETE DESEGREGATION MANDATE
(held unconstitutional)

Wright v. Council of City of Emporia, 407 U.S. 451, 92 S. Ct. 2196; *United States v. Scotland Neck City Board of Education,* 407 U.S. 484, 92 S. Ct. 2214 (1972)

The Issue. The issue in these two companion cases concerned the constitutionality of school board actions in the realignment of school districts which would tend to impede the accomplishment of complete unification of the entire district in conformity with requirements of the Fourteenth Amendment.

Background. In the *Emporia* case, the county and city had operated as one segregated school system, before federal court rulings condemned "freedom of choice" assignment plans. Thereafter the city asserted the right to operate its own school system.

Countywide, the pupil population was two-thirds black. Split systems would have produced a city district of 1,123 pupils, 48 per cent white, and a rural district 28 per cent white and 72 per cent black. Each system would have been desegregated within itself despite the disparity between districts. In essence this would have amounted to two new systems, each operating unitary schools within its borders, where one of the two systems would really be "white" and the other "Negro."

The District Court found that "in a sense, race was a factor in the city's decision to secede. The Court of Appeals for the Fourth Circuit, however, found that the primary purpose of Emporia's action was "benign" and was not "merely a cover-up" for racial discrimination.

In the *Scotland Neck* case, a state statute authorized the creation of a new school district for the city of Scotland Neck which was a part of the larger Halifax County School District, which at that time was in the process of dismantling its dual school system.

The schools of Halifax County were completely segregated by race until 1965, when the school board adopted a "freedom of choice" plan that produced a minimum of actual desegregation. In the 1967-68 school year, all the white students in the county attended the four traditionally all-white schools, while 97 per cent of the Negro students attended the 14 traditionally all-Negro schools.

In 1968, the United States Department of Justice entered into negotiations with the Halifax County School Board to bring the county's school system in compliance with federal law. Consequently an agreement was reached whereby the school board undertook to provide some desegregation in the fall of 1968 and to effect a completely unitary system in the 1969-70 school year.

An "Interim Plan" to bring about the unitary

system was introduced, but before any action had been taken on it, a bill (Chapter 31) was introduced in the state legislature to authorize the creation of a new school district bounded by the city limits of Scotland Neck. With approval of a referendum on the bill, the new district began taking steps toward beginning a separate school system in the fall of 1969. This action led to the litigation which was destined to go all the way to the United States Supreme Court.

In both the *Emporia* case and the *Scotland Neck* case, the District Court had declared the realignment of district boundaries as unconstitutional, whereas the Fourth United States Circuit Court of Appeals reversed the District Court's rulings. The United States Supreme Court then granted certiorari in both cases "to consider the circumstances under which a federal court may enjoin state or local officials from carving out a new school district from an existing district that has not yet completed the process of dismantling a system of enforced racial segregation."

U. S. Supreme Court Decisions. In both decisions the United States Supreme Court reversed the rulings of the Court of Appeals, thereby affirming those of the District Court. Although there was complete unanimity in ruling on the *Scotland Neck* case, the Justices split five to four on the *Emporia* decision. Justice Stewart, who delivered the majority opinion was joined by Justices Douglas, Brennan, White and Marshall. Joining Chief Justice Burger in a dissent, which stressed disagreement over evidence rather than principles of equality, were Justices Blackmun, Powell and Rehnquist.

In the *Emporia* case, considerable attention was focused on the "dominant purpose" of the boundary realignment. Commenting for the majority on this point, Justice Stewart stated:

> This "dominant purpose" test finds no precedent in our decisions. It is true that where an action by school authorities is motivated by a demonstrated discriminatory purpose, the existence of that purpose may add to the discriminatory effect of the action by intensifying the stigma of implied racial inferiority. And where a school board offers non-racial justifications for a plan that is less effective than other alternatives for dismantling a dual school system, a demonstrated racial purpose may be taken into consideration in determining the weight to be given to the proffered justification . . . it is difficult or impossible for any court to determine the "sole" or "dominant" motivation behind the choices of a group of legislators, and the same may be said of the choices of a school board. In addition, an inquiry into the "dominant" motivation of school authorities is as irrelevant as it is fruitless. The mandate of *Brown II* was to desegregate schools, and we have said that the measure of any desegregation plan is its effectiveness. . . . Thus, we have focused upon the effect—not the purpose or motivation—of a school board's action in determining whether it is a permissible method of dismantling a dual system. The

existence of a permissible purpose cannot sustain an action that has an impermissible effect. (92 S. Ct. at 2203)

Justice Stewart added: "Certainly, desegregation is not achieved by splitting a single school system operating 'white schools' and 'Negro schools' into two new systems, each operating unitary schools within its borders, where one of the two new systems is, in fact, 'white' and the other is, in fact 'Negro'." (*Id.* at 2204)

Justice Stewart who also delivered the opinion of the Court in the *Scotland Neck* case commented as follows:

We have today held that any attempt by state or local officials to carve out a new school district from an existing district that is in the process of dismantling a dual school system must be judged according to whether it hinders or furthers the process of school desegregation. If the proposal would impede the dismantling of a dual system, then a district court, in the exercise of its remedial discretion, may enjoin it from being carried out. The District Court in this case concluded that Chapter 31 "was enacted with the effect of creating a refuge for white students of the Halifax County School system, and interferes with the desegregation of the Halifax County School system. . . ." Our review of the record leads us to conclude that the District Court's determination was the only proper inference to be drawn from the facts of this case, and we thus reverse the judgment of the Court of Appeals. (*Id.* at 2217)

Noteworthy, in distinguishing between the two cases, and offering a rationale for the dissent in *Emporia*, are the following comments of Chief Justice Burger:

First, the operation of a separate school system in Scotland Neck would preclude meaningful desegregation in the southeastern portion of Halifax County. If Scotland Neck were permitted to operate separate schools, more than 2,200 of the nearly 3,000 students in this sector would attend virtually all-Negro schools located just outside of the corporate limits of Scotland Neck. The schools located within Scotland Neck would be predominantly white. Further shifts could reasonably be anticipated. In a very real sense, the children residing in this relatively small area would continue to attend "Negro schools" and "white schools." The effect of the withdrawal would thus be dramatically different from the effect which could be anticipated in *Emporia*.

Second, Scotland Neck's action cannot be seen as the fulfillment of its destiny as an independent governmental entity. Scotland Neck had been a part of the county-wide school system for many years; special legislation had to be pushed through the North Carolina General Assembly to enable Scotland Neck to operate its own school system. The movement toward the creation of a separate school system in Scotland Neck was prompted solely by the likelihood of desegregation in the county, not by any change in the political status of the municipality. Scotland Neck was and is a part of Halifax County. The city of Emporia, by contrast, is totally independent from Greenville County; Emporia's only ties to the county are contractual. When Emporia became a city, a status derived pursuant to long-standing statutory procedures, it took on the legal responsibility of providing for the education of its children and was no longer entitled to avail itself of the county school facilities.

Third, the District Court found, and it is undisputed, that the Scotland Neck severance was substantially motivated by the desire to create a predominantly white system more acceptable to the white parents of Scotland Neck. In other words, the new system was designed to minimize the number of Negro children attending school with the white children residing in Scotland Neck. No similar finding was made by the District Court in *Emporia*, and the record shows that Emporia's decision was not based on the projected racial composition of the proposed new system. (*Id.* at 2218-19)

Significance of the Decision. The decisions in these two companion cases are significant in several respects.

First, the United States Supreme Court affirmed the judgments of the District Court in both cases, and, thereby, reversed the judgments of the higher Court of Appeals.

Second, the decisions indicate that, although political entities are generally permitted to alter school district boundaries for legitimate reasons, the discretionary authority cannot be exercised to the extent of discrimination—particularly where race is involved.

Third, the Court leaves no doubt that realignment of school district boundaries for the purpose of maintaining some segregated schools is unconstitutional. Moreover, even where the alteration of boundaries has no racial purpose or motive, it is not judicially permissible if it impedes the establishment of unitary schools. As the Court emphasizes—ever since *Brown* II, the measure of any desegregation plan is its effectiveness regardless of purpose or motivation.

Fourth, the *Emporia* decision marks the first time, in more than eighteen years, that the Supreme Court broke ranks in a school desegregation case. Heretofore, the Court has been unanimous in its desegregation decisions. Not since before the nine to nothing *Brown* decision in 1954, outlawing state-enforced racial separation, have the justices publicly disagreed over whether a school system was complying with the equal protection clause of the Fourteenth Amendment.

Fifth, it is significant that the four dissenters in the *Emporia* case (Chief Justice Burger and Justices Blackmun, Powell and Rehnquist) were all appointees of President Nixon and are considered to be the junior members of the Court. This, however, cannot suggest that newly appointed members to the Court will result in a softer approach on civil rights. After all, the Court was unanimous in the *Scotland*

Neck decision as it was in the previous landmark *Swann* decision just one year earlier. The disagreement in *Emporia* was merely over lack of convincing evidence rather than principles of equality.

Chapter 25

CONCLUSIONS AND IMPLICATIONS

The selected landmark decisions of the United States Supreme Court affecting the public schools have been presented in this report in chronological order. However, for purposes of stating conclusions and implications of the decisions which have been analyzed, it is considered better to treat them categorically. By so doing, the seven arbitrarily-chosen categories are: (1) curriculum, (2) compulsory school attendance, (3) teachers' right of association, (4) teachers' right of expression, (5) desegregation of races, (6) due process rights of students, and (7) parochiaid. Admittedly, this classification does not result in an even distribution of decisions in the various categories. As many as eight United States Supreme Court decisions fall in the broad category of (1) curriculum; whereas only one decision constitutes an entire category in two instances.

Curriculum

Statutory Prohibition to Teach German. The very first landmark decision referred to in this report dealt with a curriculum matter. The main issue, however, concerned the academic freedom of teachers and the right of parents to determine the instruction of their children. The Court was not concerned with the subject matter (German, *per se*) but rather with violation of the "due process" clause of the Fourteenth Amendment. The Court held that the statute prohibiting the teaching of German did not fall within the police power of the state, and that it denied the right of the teacher to teach that subject for which he was professionally prepared, and the right of parents to engage him so for the instruction of their children—all of which was clearly violative of the due process clause of the Fourteenth Amendment.

Flag-salute Requirement. One of the most hotly-contested and litigated curriculum issues had to do with the flag-salute requirement. For many years the Jehovah's Witnesses protested the regulation with the contention that it violated their freedom of religion rights contained in the First Amendment of the United States Constitution.

After receiving adverse decisions from state courts, Gobitis appealed the case (*Minersville School District* v. *Gobitis,* 1940) to the United States Supreme Court which upheld a state court ruling to the effect that it was within the school board's authority to require the flag salute as a means of achieving a feeling of national unity.

The most significant aspect of the *Gobitis* case was the strong dissenting opinion which, later, in *Barnette* became the majority opinion. So finally the High Court ruled that the flag-salute requirement in the public schools was a violation of the First Amendment rights contained in the Constitution.

Apparently the decision in the *West Virginia State Board of Education* v. *Barnette,* 1943 case settled the flag-salute controversy—at least as far as the courts are concerned. Although the issue has since been litigated in the lower courts, the rulings have followed the legal precedent established in *Barnette*.

Released Time for Religious Instruction. Having been rigidly limited in the extent to which religious instruction could be carried on in regular classes, certain religious groups (Protestants, Catholics, and Jews) sought to have religion taught in the schools on a released-time basis.

In the first case (*McCollum v. Board of Education*, 1948) reaching the Supreme Court on the issue, the Court ignored the contentions of the religious groups that (1) the program was voluntary, (2) the use of schoolrooms for the classes did not amount to financial support, and (3) the teachers were not paid for out of public school funds. The thrust of the High Court's decision was that the mingling of religious education in the public schools during public school time, as was done in the Champaign city schools, was in conflict with the First Amendment.

Several years later the issue was litigated again in the New York case (*Zorach v. Clauson*, 1952) but under different circumstances. The United States Supreme Court agreed with the state court and upheld the New York program of released time on the grounds that there was neither supervision nor approval of religious teachers and no solicitation of pupils or distribution of cards; the religious instruction had to be outside the school building and grounds; and that there could be no announcement of any kind in the public schools relative to the program, and no comment by any principal or teacher on the attendance or nonattendance of any pupil.

Although strong dissenting opinions were presented in the *Zorach* decision, the issue on released time has simmered down. Apparently parents are not anxious to have their children transferred from school buildings to religious centers for sectarian instruction during regular school hours. The "shared-time" arrangement appears to be a preferable alternative.

Requirement for Recitation of State Prayer. The practice of reciting brief prayers as a part of opening exercises had been carried on in many places for many years. The constitutionality of the practice, however, was not seriously challenged until (*Engel* v. *Vitale*, 1962) when the New York State Board of Regents composed a brief prayer to be recited in the public schools of New York.

The Court of Appeals of New York State held the recitation of the regents' prayer as required by the school district was legal. On appeal, however, the United States Supreme Court ruled otherwise and ruled that the required recitation of the mandated prayer was inconsistent with the Establishment Clause of the First Amendment. Significantly, nothing in the Court's decision indicated that *voluntary* prayers were illegal.

Although there was only one dissenting opinion in the decision, the repercussions throughout the nation have been tremendous. Many attempts have been made to circumvent the ruling—even to the extent of amending the Constitution—but so far the courts have held firm to the precedent established in *Engel* v. *Vitale*.

Requirement to Read Passages from the Bible. Just one year after the United States Supreme Court decision invalidating the recitations of mandated prayers, the constitutionality of another religious practice—the reading of passages from the Bible—was tested by the Supreme Court in *Abington* v. *Schempp*, (1963).

In conformity with the ruling laid down in the prayer case, the Court invalidated a Pennsylvania statute that required the reading of at least ten verses from the Holy Bible at the opening exercises of each public school. Since the statute required the reading of the *Holy Bible*, a *Christian document*, the Court detected a preference for the Christian religion and therefore a violation of the Establishment Clause of the First Amendment.

Nothing in the decision indicates that the Bible may not be used as a document for secular educational purposes. The Court distinguished between the *legal* practice of teaching *about religion* and the *illegal* teaching *of religion*.

Statutory Prohibition to Teach Theory of Evolution. For nearly a half century legislators, school officials, teachers, and parents had been in a quandry regarding the legality of having the theory of evolution (Darwinism) taught in the public schools. The famous Scopes case of 1927 established a precedent which was to be followed for more than forty years, which, in essence, meant that although one's right to oppose the anti-evolution law elsewhere, that right did not extend to public school teachers in the classroom.

Even as late as 1968, in the *Epperson* v. *Arkansas*, the Supreme Court of Arkansas held firm to the earlier-established principle that the anti-evolution law was a valid exercise of the state's power to specify the curriculum in the public schools. On appeal, however, the United States Supreme Court overturned the state ruling on the grounds that the state's undoubted right to prescribe the curriculum does not carry with it the right to prohibit the teaching of a scientific theory or doctrine where the prohibition is based upon reasons that violate the First Amendment.

That the High Court's ruling in *Epperson* is now firmly established is evidenced in the decision of *Smith* v. *State* (1970) where the State Supreme Court of Mississippi held that the anti-evolution statutes of that state "are in contravention of the First Amendment to the Constitution of the United States" as laid down in *Epperson*.

Compulsory School Attendance

Public School Attendance Requirement. Much of the early litigation concerning schools had to do with compulsory school attendance. Although compulsory attendance was generally accepted, there were differences of opinion as to whether the attendance had to be at a *public* school. Many parents wished for their children to attend a private (parochial) school; whereas others feared such choice would cause divisiveness of the American public school system and jeopardize its effectiveness.

The issue was carried to the United States Supreme Court in 1925 where the Oregon case (*Pierce* v. *Society*) was tested. Litigation on the case emanated from an Oregon law requiring children between the ages of eight and sixteen to attend *public* schools.

In a unanimous decision, the High Court held that the Oregon law was unconstitutional and referred to the provisions of the Fourteenth Amendment as nullifying legislation designed to "deprive any person of life, liberty, or property without due process of law." Undoubtedly a contrary decision would have done away with the nonpublic school systems throughout the nation.

The precedential consequence of the decision in *Pierce* v. *Society* is indicated by the frequency to which it is referred in subsequent cases involving parental versus state authority over the pupil.

Compulsory School Attendance of Amish Children. Until 1972, the courts were consistent in ruling that compulsory school attendance laws *were not* in conflict with the First and Fourteenth Amendments to the United States Constitution when parents refused to send their children to school because of religious beliefs. However, the United States Supreme Court veered away from this long-accepted legal principle in *Wisconsin* v. *Yoder* (1972)—at least as it applied to Amish children who had completed the elementary grades.

In this case the Court reasoned that the effect of

exemptions to the compulsory school attendance law of Wisconsin would "do no more to the ultimate goal of education than to dent the symmetry of the design for enforcement." The Court emphasized, however, that exemption applied only to the Amish because of their proven sincerity to the belief that the educational requirement was in conflict with their religious views and that their alternative program was one which other religious groups would be unlikely to duplicate.

The most logical criticism of the decision in *Wisconsin* v. *Yoder* is that, since a significant number of Amish children leave the Old Order and their homeland, the children, rather than the parents, should have a voice in their educational future. As Justice Douglas warns that if the child "is harnessed to the Amish way of life by those in authority over him and if his education is truncated, his entire life may be stunted and deformed."

Teachers' Right of Association

Although there is no *direct* provision in our national constitution pertaining to the right of association for teachers, that right for teachers, as well as for all other citizens, is a part of our democratic society, and, by implication, has a definite place in American constitutional law through "right of assembly" and "due process" concepts.

Dismissal of Teachers for Refusal to Comply with Oath Requirements. In the first case (*Adler* v. *Board of Education*, 1952) reaching the United States Supreme Court which dealt with the issue, the Court upheld the school board's dismissal of teachers for refusal to comply with the oath requirements as stipulated by the famous Feinberg Law. In the six to three decision, the Court reasoned that since the teacher works in a sensitive area where the attitudes of young minds toward the society in which they live, "school authorities have the right and duty to screen the officials, teachers, and employees as to their fitness to maintain the integrity of the schools as a part of ordered society."

Dismissal for Refusal to Reveal Association. Six years after *Adler*, the United States Supreme Court was called upon again to settle an issue concerning "right of association" in the case of *Beilan* v. *Board of Education* (1958). In this case the teacher invoked the Fifth Amendment and refused to answer questions of the school administrators regarding alleged association with the Communist Political Association. The dismissal of the teacher was upheld by a bare majority of the Court on the ground of "incompetency" as conceived in the Pennsylvania statutes.

Although the Court ruled that Beilan's discharge *did not* violate the due process clause of the Fourteenth Amendment, the four dissenting judges took sharp issue with the majority opinion. The unpopularity of the *Beilan* decision presaged an eventual reversal of judicial rulings on issues involving teachers' association with subversive organizations. Decisions on the next two cases to be reported confirm this contention.

Oath Requirement of Non-affiliation with

Subversive Organizations. The United States Supreme Court, in another five to four decision, invalidated an Arizona Act requiring an oath from state employees (including public school teachers) that they were not knowingly members of the Communist Party or a subversive organization. The Court was reluctant to penalize the teachers in this case (*Elfbrandt* v. *Russell*, 1966) who refused to sign the oath because of its vagueness. Moreover, the Court held that a law cannot stand that rests on "guilt by association." A law which applies to membership without specific intent to further the illegal aims of the organization is considered by the Court to infringe "unnecessarily on protected freedoms."

Dismissal of Teacher for Refusal to Sign Affidavit of Non-affiliation with Communist Party. The decision in *Keyishian* v. *Board of Regents* (1967) overturned the Feinberg Law which had been in effect for a quarter of a century. Among other stipulations, the law provided that membership in a listed subversive organization "shall constitute prima facie evidence for disqualification for appointment to or retention in any office or position in the school system."

As in the previous case (*Elfbrandt*), the Court again ruled that the law was vague. Also, the Court was of the opinion that it is necessary to safeguard academic freedom of teachers—which is a special concern of the First Amendment.

Although there is a definite lack of judicial unanimity regarding the constitutionality of laws requiring the signing of oaths of non-affiliation with subversive organizations, or the dismissal of those who refuse to sign the oaths, the trend appears to be that *membership* in itself is not to be outlawed. Subversive *action* on the part of those who are members, however, is not likely to be judicially condoned.

Teachers' Right of Public Expression

Teachers, as well as other citizens, have the constitutional right to express themselves on matters which are of concern to the public—providing the expressions are not injurious to others. In the case of teachers, the expression is unlawful if it proves to be detrimental to the pupil or disruptive to the educative process.

Dismissal of Teacher for Expression of Public Concern. In a landmark decision (*Pickering* v. *Board of Education,* 1968), the United States Supreme Court reversed a judgment of the Supreme Court of Illinois which had upheld the dismissal of a teacher (Pickering) by the school board for sending a letter to a local newspaper concerning a proposed tax increase.

The letter severely criticized the school board and the superintendent for the manner in which they had previously handled proposals to raise and use new revenue. However, since there was no proof that the letter resulted in injury to the pupils or the educative process the Court could find no legitimate reason for dismissing the teacher. Consequently, the dismissal was held to violate the right of free speech as guaranteed by the First Amendment.

A significant implication of the Court's ruling is that teachers have a *preferential right* to express themselves on school issues, as is indicated by the following passage:

> Teachers are, as a class, the members of a community most likely to have informed and definite opinions as to how funds allotted to the operation of the school should be spent. Accordingly, it is essential that they be able to speak out freely, on such questions without fear of retaliatory dismissal.

Desegregation

Segregation of the Races in the Public Schools. For those who had been watching "the writing on the wall" there was no great surprise in the decision of the *Brown* case. Earlier decisions in the *Sweatt* and *McLaurin* cases gave warning that the same legal principles involving institutions of higher learning would ultimately be extended downward to include public elementary and secondary schools. Nevertheless, when the United States Supreme Court rendered a unanimous decision outlawing segregation of white and Negro children in the public schools solely on the basis of race, the public appeared to be stunned.

In essence the *Brown* decision discarded the "separate but equal" principle laid down in *Plessy* v. *Ferguson*, in 1896, in lieu of the more modern principle that, even though the physical facilities and other tangible factors be equal, the segregation of white and Negro children in the public schools denies the Negro children the equal protection of the laws guaranteed by the Fourteenth Amendment.

While the Court was unanimous in its opinion, the same degree of unanimity was by no means expressed by the public. Consequently, the second *Brown* case was initiated in 1955 for implementation of the *Brown I* decision. Despite the Court's decision in *Brown I* and the guidelines laid down in *Brown II*, it was obvious that litigation on the issue was not concluded, as subsequent landmark decisions reveal.

Defiance of Desegregation Order. The *Cooper* v. *Aaron* case of 1958 was prompted by the blatant opposition of the Arkansas Legislature and Governor to comply with the Federal Court order to desegregate the races in the public schools in accordance with the *Brown* decisions.

There have been very few cases, if any, where the United States Supreme Court has expressed itself with more force and candor in ruling against those who defy the federal government. The judicial lash was not spared in pointing out that the power of the State Legislature and Governor of Arkansas was being used to thwart law rather than sustaining it, as indicated by the following succinct statement: "For those in authority thus to defy the law of the land is profoundly subversive not only of our constitutional system but of the presuppositions of a democratic society."

Nevertheless, state actions concerning desegregation are continuously being enacted, even though they are contrary to federal laws—perhaps not so directly as those displayed by the Arkansas officials, but with the same purposes of circumventing Supreme Court decisions.

Busing of Students to Achieve Racial Balance. The *Brown* decision of 1954 left no doubt that the dual system of racially desegregated schools was unconstitutional and would therefore have to be terminated. Virtually all attempts to develop a unitary system have met with opposition of the diehards. The most violent opposition has been focused on busing of pupils to achieve racial balance. Nevertheless, the decision in *Swann* (1971) upheld busing as a legal tool to dismantle the dual system *immediately* and *completely*. The Court made it clear, however, that massive busing of pupils would not have to be resorted to if other alternative legal tools for dismantling the dual system were effectively applied.

Before condemning busing of pupils, it should be noted that the practice is not new. With the consolidation of small school systems and the increasing hazards of traffic, busing has been considered, for several decades, essential. Moreover, before *Brown*, many Negro children were transported by bus, past nearby white schools to take them to all-Negro schools which were much further away in distance.

The most valid criticism of busing is when *young* children are transported *great* distances to achieve racial balance. That the Court was aware of this is indicated by its statement: "An objection to transportation of students may have validity when the time or distance of travel is so great as to either risk the health of the children or significantly impinge on the educational process." Accordingly "district courts must weigh the soundness of any transportation plan."

If the attempts to overturn the decision in *Swann* should be successful, other alternative tools for dismantling the dual school systems would likely meet with opposition and resentment also—which raises the question as to whether all the agitation is over busing *per se* or over desegregation.

Alteration of School Boundaries to Avoid Complete Desegregation Mandate. Altering district boundaries is a well-recognized stratagem to perpetuate racial segregation in certain localities. However, neither the realignment of an attendance district nor of an administrative district is constitutionally permissible if the purpose or effect is to impede desegregation of the races in the public schools. In the eyes of the Court, that which cannot be legally accomplished directly cannot be accomplished indirectly.

Even where the alteration of boundaries has no racial purpose or motive, it is not judicially permissible if it impedes the establishment of unitary schools. This implication is evident in the Court's statement concerning the two companion cases (*Emporia* and *Scotland Neck*, 1972): "The existence of a permissible purpose cannot sustain an action that has an impermissible effect."

Parochiaid

Free Textbooks for Parochial Pupils. Although "parochiaid" is a relatively-new term its meaning was obvious and applicable as early as 1930 when the United States Supreme Court upheld the constitutionality of a Louisiana Act which authorized the appropriation of public funds for textbooks to *all* children of the state—which included children attending nonpublic schools.

The decision in this textbook case (*Cochran* v. *Louisiana*, 1930) marked the beginning of the so-called "child benefit theory," which, in essence, meant the textbooks were being furnished free to the parochial pupils for their benefit, with only a "resulting benefit of the state."

Despite much opposition to the decision, because of its opening the door to the public treasury, the legal principle it established has perpetuated through the years.

Free Transportation for Parochial Pupils. An expansion of the "child benefit theory" occurred seventeen years after the textbook decision when the United States Supreme Court validated a provision of a New Jersey statute, and thereby sustained the right of local school authorities to provide free transportation for pupils attending parochial schools. The line of reasoning in the Court's five to four decision was much the same as that manifested earlier in the Louisiana textbook decision.

It was argued by the dissenting judges that the judicial reasoning expressed in both the textbook case and the pupil transportation case might well encourage certain nonpublic schools to seek extension of public expenditures to cover many other costs associated with education. It is well recognized that public assumption of any phase of nonpublic school expenses reduces the costs which would otherwise have to be borne by the nonpublic schools themselves.

Allocation of Public Funds for Nonpublic Schools. The *indirect* public aid provided to parochial schools as a result of the "child benefit" decisions, coupled with the economic plight of parochial schools in a period of rising costs, presaged eventual attempts to secure more *direct* public aid for parochial schools.

The constitutionality of such attempts was tested in the *Lemon* v. *Kurtzman* (Pa.) and *Earley* v. *Di Censo* (R.I.) cases in 1971. The Rhode Island Act sought salary supplements for teachers of secular subjects in nonpublic schools, whereas the Pennsylvania Act sought reimbursement to nonpublic schools for teachers' salaries, textbooks and instructional materials to be used in the teaching of specific secular subjects.

The United States Supreme Court held that both statutes were unconstitutional under the religious clauses of the First Amendment, even though promoting secular purposes. In its decision, the Court stressed that the programs for which *direct* aid was sought would involve "excessive entanglement between government and religion."

It is quite probable that hereafter any further attempts for parochial financial aid—whether direct or indirect—will be measured by the rulings in these two precedential decisions. In fact, in a later case (*Wolman* v. *Essex*, 1972) a federal court ruled that an Ohio statute which authorized grants to reimburse parents for tuition of nonpublic school children violated the ·establishment clause." **N.B.** On October 10, 1972, the United States Supreme Court affirmed the lower court's ruling. (The Ohio plan had been considered a testing ground for new methods of public aid to church-related schools.)

Also the United States Supreme Court agreed to review, during the 1973 session, various methods in New York and Pennsylvania of providing state aid to parochial schools. The Ohio Legislature should have anticipated such a ruling in the light of the earlier *Lemon* decision.

Due Process Rights of Students

Students' Right to Express Symbolic Expression. In recent years, high-school students and others have adopted various methods of symbolic expression against "the establishment." Judging from the number of court cases arising from symbolic expressions, those pertaining to hair styles of boys top the list. Of more than a hundred reported hair style cases, the majority have been settled in state courts or federal courts below the Supreme Court level—much to the relief of the United States Supreme Court.

Other methods of symbolic expression included the wearing of armbands and freedom buttons as protest gestures against governmental involvement in the Vietnam hostilities. The one landmark United States Supreme Court decision on the issue grew out of the much-publicized *Tinker* case of Des Moines. As has been described in the discussion of this case, the Tinker children were suspended from school for their refusal to remove black armbands which were worn to publicize objections to the United States involvement in Vietnam.

Although a United States District Court upheld the school authorities' action—"based upon the fear of disturbance from wearing the armbands"—the United States Supreme Court reversed the lower court decision. The Court's rationale was that the students' symbolic expression was akin to free speech and therefore fell within the rights of the Free Speech Clause of the First Amendment. Since *all* citizens enjoy the guarantee of the Constitution it cannot be denied to students in the public schools.

Of course when it can be proved that the wearing of protest insignia or any other symbolic expression is disruptive to the school, the Court may decide that the interest of the State is superior to "the untrammeled exercise of speech, symbolic or otherwise."

Forthcoming Landmark Decisions

In all probability more landmark decisions will be rendered by the United States Supreme Court during subsequent years—perhaps even before this publication is released from the press. On the basis of present controversy and agitation, more litigation may be anticipated by the courts all the way through the highest court in the land. Issues concerning school prayers, parochiaid, and busing of pupils will likely come up again for judicial review, and, since they involve provisions of the federal Constitution, they could conceivably be considered and ruled upon by the Supreme Court.

However, the most likely area for prompt United States Supreme Court consideration has to do with the constitutionality of the local property tax as a source of school revenue. National attention was given to this issue when, in the *Serrano* v. *Priest* case (487 P.2d 1241, 1971), the Supreme Court of California held that the public school financing system of that state, which relies heavily on the local property tax for school revenue, causes substantial disparities among individual school students in the amount of revenue available per pupil. In its lengthy report the California Court stated:

> We have determined that this funding scheme indiviously [sic] discriminates against the poor because it makes the quality of a child's education a function of wealth of his parents and neighbors. Recognizing as we must that the right to an education in our public schools is a fundamental interest which cannot be conditioned on wealth, we can discern no compelling state purpose necessitating the present method of financing. We have concluded therefore, that such a system cannot withstand constitutional challenge and must fall before the equal protection clause. (*Id.* at 1244)

At the time of this writing, rulings similar to that in the California case have been rendered by state and federal courts in Arizona, Minnesota, New Jersey, Texas, and Wyoming. It had been assumed by many that the *Serrano* decision would be the first appealed to the United States Supreme Court. Reportedly, however, the case which the Supreme Court has agreed to rule upon in its 1972-73 term is one that originated in Texas (*Rodriguez* v. *San Antonio Independent School District*, 337 F. Supp. 280, U.S.D.C. W.D. Texas 1971).

With language strikingly similar to that used in *Serrano*, the district court stated:

> Having determined that the current system of financing public education in Texas discriminates on the basis of wealth by permitting citizens of affluent districts to provide a higher quality education for their children, while paying lower taxes, this Court concludes, as a matter of law, that the plaintiffs have been denied equal protection of the laws under the Fourteenth Amendment to the United States Constitution. . . . (*Id.* at 285)

Should the United States Supreme Court uphold the decision in *Rodriguez* the effect would be tremendous in the many other states that rely heavily upon the local property tax as a source of school revenue. Hopefully, a substitutional method of financing the public schools could prove to be more equitable and democratic.

TABLE OF CASES

---

* Denotes selected landmark cases.

*Everson v. Board of Education (N.J.), 330 U.S. 1, 67 S. Ct. 504 (1947), p. 53.

Frain v. Baron (N.Y.), 307 F. Supp. 27 (1969), p. 50.

Green v. County School Board (Va.), 391 U.S. 430, 88 S. Ct. 1689 (1968), p. 179.

Hill v. Lewis (N.C.), 323 F. Supp. 55 (1971), p. 169.

Kaplan v. School District of Philadelphia, 388 Pa. 213, 130 A.2d 672 (1957), p. 110.

*Keyishian v. Board of Regents (N.Y.), 385 U.S. 589, 87 S. Ct. 675 (1967), p. 137.

*Lemon v. Kurtzman (Pa.), 403 U.S. 602, 91 S. Ct. 2105 (1971), p. 171.

Los Angeles Teachers Union v. Los Angeles City Board of Education, 78 Cal. Rptr. 723 (1969), p. 150.

*McCollum v. Board of Education (Ill.), 333 U.S. 203, 68 S. Ct. 461 (1948), p. 65.

*Meyer v. Nebraska, 262 U.S. 390, 43 S. Ct. 625 (1923), p. 11.

Meyer v. State, 107 Neb. 657, 187 N.W. 100 (1922), p. 13.

*Minersville School District v. Gobitis (Pa.), 310 U.S. 586, 60 S. Ct. 1010 (1940), p. 33.

Murray v. Curlett, Constituting the Board of School Commissioners of Baltimore City, 228 Md. 239, 179 A.2d 698 (1962), p. 122.

*Pickering v. Board of Education (Ill.), 391 U.S. 563, 88 S. Ct. 1731 (1968), p. 145.

*Pierce v. Society of Sisters (Ore.), 268 U.S. 510, 45 S. Ct. 571 (1925), p. 19.

Plessy v. Ferguson (La.), 16 S. Ct. 1138 (1896), p. 89.

Rodriguez v. San Antonio Independent School District (Tex.), 337 F. Supp. 280 (1971), p. 229.

Serrano v. Priest (Cal.), 487 P.2d 1241 (1971), p. 228.

Smith v. State (Miss.), 242 So. 2d 692 (1970), p. 158.

State v. Lundquist, 262 Md. 534, 278 A.2d 263 (1971), p. 51.

State v. Yoder, 49 Wis. 2d 430, 182 N.W.2d 539 (1971), p. 190.

---

* Denotes selected landmark cases.

---

* Denotes selected landmark cases.